The Person and
Work of the
Holy Spirit

OTHER WARFIELD TITLES
FROM SOLID GROUND

In addition to *The Person and Work of the Holy Spirit* Solid Ground has also published the following books by B.B. Warfield:

Biblical and Theological Studies: *Addresses on the 100th Anniversary of Princeton Theological Seminary in 1912* by Allis, Machen, Wilson, Vos, Warfield and more.

Princeton Sermons from 1891-92 by Aiken, Green, Hodge, Patton, Aiken, Warfield and more.

The Lord of Glory: *Classic Defense of the Deity of Christ* by B.B. Warfield

The Power of God unto Salvation: *Chapel Sermons from Princeton Seminary* by B.B. Warfield

Calvin Memorial Addresses: *Celebrating the 400th Anniversary of the Birth of John Calvin* by Warfield, Johnson, Orr, Webb and more

The Person and Work of the Holy Spirit

Benjamin B. Warfield

SOLID GROUND CHRISTIAN BOOKS
BIRMINGHAM, ALABAMA USA
205-443-0311

Solid Ground Christian Books
PO Box 660132
Vestavia Hills AL 35266
205-443-0311
sgcb@charter.net
solid-ground-books.com

ISBN: 978-159925-146-2

Cover Design by Borgo Design, Tuscaloosa. Alabama.
Contact them at borgogirl@bellsouth.net

Acknowledgements

The Editor, Michael Gaydosh, would like to thank *Gary Hough*, who
first introduced him to the writings of Warfield; *William Harris*, for
his enthusiasm and help on this project as librarian of Princeton
Seminary; *Sinclair Ferguson*, for his support of this project from its
inception; and *Ruth Baldwin* and *Newton Bush* for their valuable
assistance on this work.

Warfield, Benjamin B., 1851-1921—
   The Person and Work of the Holy Spirit
Recommended Dewey Decimal Classification: 234
Suggested Subject Headings:
1. Religion—Christian literature—The Holy Spirit
2. Christianity—The Holy Spirit—Benjamin B. Warfield
3. The Bible—The Holy Spirit—teaching literature.
I. Title

Manufactured in the United States of America

Table of Contents

SERMONS

ARTICLES

BOOK REVIEWS

Introductory Word

B.B. Warfield (1851-1921) is best known as one of the towering geniuses in the last one hundred years of American church life. Born near Lexington, Kentucky, he graduated from both the University and the Seminary at Princeton and in 1887 returned to the Seminary as a theology professor.

Warfield wrote a number of books on a variety of subjects. After his death, Oxford University Press published a magnificent ten volume set of his articles. These, as well as several of his books, have been reprinted. More recently a further two volumes of his shorter writings have also been published. Thus, seventy years after his death, his writings are probably more widely read and appreciated than ever.

The range and penetration of Warfield's knowledge is breathtaking: he was a skilled New Testament scholar, a patient historian, a widely read theologian, and a learned controversialist. All this was married to an easy style which guaranteed that his work can be read today with pleasure.

These qualities are the fruit of living in a community of Christian scholars, as Warfield did at Princeton. Here he enjoyed many uninterrupted hours of study, reflection, and writing. But his life was not free from personal burden and inner pain. Shortly after his marriage, Warfield and his wife were caught in a thunderstorm. The severity of it had an overpowering and debilitating effect on Mrs. Warfield and left her virtually an invalid for the rest of her life. Her husband thereafter allowed his life and work to be circumscribed by her condition and rarely seems to have left her side for periods of any length. In the providence of God, however, this limitation on his movements became the plowed field in which the seed thoughts of his fertile mind grew into the harvest of scholarly articles and books he later wrote.

Warfield, however, was not *exclusively* a scholar. Indeed, for all his learning, he was not even *primarily* a scholar. He was first and foremost a Christian and a minister of the gospel. Thus, in addition to the instruction of the class, he also preached. And what material!— as will soon become obvious from this volume, which is largely composed of a selection of his sermons.

Of course, these sermons could only have been composed by a scholar. Yet they are not scholastic. Admittedly, they also demanded more from their hearers than the well-packaged, story-dominated sermons of our own day; but they were magnificently crafted, and full of biblical protein for the mind and heart. There is nothing eccentric in them; they exude grace. Our own efforts today seem weak, and yes, ugly, by comparison.

Nowhere is this more true than in teaching and preaching about the Holy Spirit,— the theme of these chapters. Much of our contemporary interest in the Spirit seems to miss the real point of His coming and the central blessings of His ministry. Here Warfield not only redresses that balance; he gives mature instruction, wonderful insight, and, at times, breathtakingly beautiful exposition. These are pages to ponder and treasure.

Such a recommendation is, clearly, the testimony of an enthusiast. Indeed, but only because like a multitude of others, I have come to appreciate the great gift Warfield was to the Christian Church.

I well remember the first time I heard Warfield's name. I was seventeen and a shy Scottish University freshman who was being engaged in conversation by an older and (it seemed) infinitely more knowledgeable student from England. He made mention of Warfield as though he were a household word. I had never heard of anyone with that name. But, whoever this Warfield might have been, I there and then determined I would know something about him before the next time I heard his name. Once is enough to feel completely ignorant! And so began a growing appreciation of a master theologian.

I commend these pages, then, as one who has again and again been helped by their contents. **Solid Ground**, under Michael Gaydosh's inspiration, has put us all in its debt by publishing this fine selection of Warfield's material on the person and ministry of the Holy Spirit. It is a treasure to be read and enjoyed again and again. If you have never made Warfield's acquaintance before, this is an ideal place to begin. With so much of his writing still readily available, I think it is safe to predict that it will be the first of many profitable meetings.

Sinclair B. Ferguson
Westminster Theological Seminary
Philadelphia, Pennsylvania USA

SERMONS

1

OLD TESTAMENT RELIGION

Psalm 51:12a: "Restore unto me the joy of Thy salvation."

"And David said unto Nathan, 'I have sinned against the Lord.' And Nathan said unto David, 'The Lord also hath put away thy sin'" (2 Sam. 12:13). It may almost seem that David escaped from his crime too easily. We may read the narrative and fail to observe the signs of that deep contrition which such hideous wickedness, when once recognized, surely must engender. There is the story of the sin drawn in all its shocking details. Then Nathan comes in with his beautiful apologue of the ewe-lamb, and its pungent application. And then we read simply: "And David said unto Nathan, 'I have sinned against the Lord.' And Nathan said unto David, 'The Lord also hath put away thy sin.'" After that comes only the story of how the child of sin was smitten, and how David besought the Lord for its life and finally acquiesced in the divine judgment. One is apt to feel that David was more concerned to escape the consequences of his sin than to yield to the Lord the sacrifices of a broken and a contrite heart. Does it not seem cold to us and external, David's simple acknowledgment of his sin and the Lord's immediate remission of it? We feel the lack of the manifestations of a deeply repentant spirit, and are almost ready, we say, to wonder if David did not escape too easily from the evil he had wrought.

The Holy Spirit

It is merely the simplicity of the narrative which is deceiving us in this. The single-hearted writer expects us to read into the bare words of David's confession, "I have sinned against the Lord," all the spiritual exercises which those words are fitted to suggest and out of which they should have grown. And if we find it a little difficult to do so, we have only to turn to David's penitential psalms to learn the depths of repentance which wrung this great and sensitive soul. One of them— perhaps the most penetrating portrayal of a truly penitent soul ever cast into human speech— is assigned by its title[1] to just this crisis in his life; and I see no good reason why this assignment need be questioned. The whole body of them sound the depths of the sinful soul's self-torment and longing for recovery as can be found nowhere else in literature; and taken in sequence present a complete portrayal of the course of repentance in the heart, from its inception in the rueful review of the past and the remorseful biting back of the awakened heart, through its culmination in a true return to God in humble love and trusting confidence, to its issue in the establishment of a new relation of obedience to God and a new richness of grateful service to Him.

Let us take just these four, Psalms 6, 38, 51, 32. In Psalm 6 sounds the note of remorse— it is the torment of a soul's perception of its sin that is here prominently brought to our most poignant observation. In Psalm 38, the note of hope— not indeed absent even from Psalm 6— becomes dominant, and the sorrow and hatred of sin is colored by a pervasive tone of relief. In Psalm 51, while there is no lessening of the accent of repentance, there is, along with the deep sense of the guilt and pollution of sin which is expressed, also a note of triumph over the sin, which aspires to a clean heart and a steadfast spirit and a happy service of God in purity of life. While in Psalm 32, the sense of forgiveness, the experience of joy in the Lord, and the exercises of holy and joyful service overlie all else. Here we trace David's penitent soul through all its experiences: his remorseful contemplation of his own sin, his passionate reaching out to the salvation of God, the gradual return of his experience of the joy of that salvation, his final issuing into the full glory of its complete realization. In some respects, the most remarkable of this remarkable body of pictures of the inner experiences of a penitent soul is that of Psalm 51. It draws away the veil for us and permits us to look in upon the spirit in the most characteristic act of repentance, just at the turning point, as it deserts its sin and turns to God. Here is revealed to us a sense of sin so poignant, a perception of the grace of God so soaring, an apprehension of the completeness of the revolution required in sinful man that he may become in any worthy sense a servant of God so profound, that one wonders in reading it what is left for a specifically Christian experience to add to this experience of a saint of God under the Old Testament dispensation in turning from sin to God. The wonderful depth of the religious experience and the remarkable richness of religious conception embodied in this psalm have indeed proved a snare to the critics. "David could not have had these ideas," says Prof. T. C. Cheyne[2], brusquely; and, indeed, the David that Prof. Cheyne has constructed out of his imaginary reconstruction of the course of religious development in Israel, could not well have had these ideas. These are distinctively Christian ideas that the psalm sets forth, and they could not have grown up of themselves in a purely natural heart. And therein lies one of the values of the psalm to us; it reveals to us the essentially Christian type of the religion of Israel; it opens to our observation the contents of the mind and heart of a Spirit-led child of God in the ages gone by, and makes us to know the truly Christian character of his experiences in his struggle with sin and his aspirations toward God, and thus also to know the supernatural leading of God's people through all ages.

For consider for a moment the conception of God which throbs through all the passionate language of this psalm. A God of righteousness who will not look upon sin with allowance; nay, who directs all things, even the emergence of acts of sin in His world, so that He may not only be just, but also "may be justified when He speaks and clear when He judges" (Psalm 51:4b). A God of holiness whose Spirit cannot abide in our impure hearts. A God of unbounded power, who governs the whole course of events in accordance with His own counsels. But above all, a gracious God, full of lovingkindness, abundant in compassion, whose delight is in salvation. There is nothing here which goes beyond the great revelation of Exodus 34:6, "a God full of compassion and gracious, abundant in lovingkindness and truth; keeping lovingkindness for thousands, forgiving iniquity and transgression and sin." Indeed the language of the psalm is obviously modeled on this of Exodus. But here it is not given from the lips of Jehovah, proclaiming His character, but is returned to us from the heart of the repentant sinner, recounting the nature of the God with whom he has to do.

And what a just and profound sense of sin is revealed to us here. The synonymy of the subject is almost exhausted in the effort to complete the self-accusation. "My transgression, my iniquity, my sin;" I have been in rebellion against God, I have distorted my life, I have missed the mark; I have, to express it all, done what is evil in Thy sight— in the sight of Thee, the Standard of Holiness, the hypostatized Law of Conduct. And these acts are but the expression of an inner nature of corruption, inherited from those who have gone before me; it was in iniquity that I was born, in sin that my mother conceived me. Shall a pure thing come from an impure? Nay, my overt acts of sin are thought of not in themselves but as manifestations of what is behind and within; thrown up into these manifestations in act, in Thine own ordinance, for no other cause than that Thy righteous condemnation on me may be justified and Thy judgment be made clear. For it is not cleanness of act merely that Thou dost desire, but truth in the inward parts and wisdom in the hidden parts. Obviously the psalmist is conceiving sin here as not confined to acts but consisting essentially of a great ocean of sin within us, whose waves merely break in sinful acts. No wonder the commentators remark that here we have original sin "more distinctly expressed than in any other passage in the Old Testament." Nothing is left to be added by the later revelation in the way of poignancy of conception— though much is, of course, left to be added in developed statement.

Accordingly, the conception of the radical nature of the operation required for the psalmist's deliverance from sin is equally developed. No surface remedy will suffice to eradicate a sin which is thus inborn, ingrained in nature itself. Hence the passionate cry: "Create"— it requires nothing less than a creative act— "Create me a clean heart"— the heart is the totality of the inner life— "and make new within me a constant spirit"— a spirit which will no more decline from Thee. Nothing less than this will suffice— a total rebegetting, as the New Testament would put it; an entire making over again can alone suffice to make such an one as the psalmist knows himself to be— not by virtue of his sins of act which are only the manifestation of what he is by nature, but by virtue of his fundamental character— acceptable to Him who desires truth in the inward part; nay, nothing less than this can secure to him that steadfastness of spirit which will save his overt acts from shame.

Nor does the psalmist expect to be able, unaided, to live in the power of his new life. One of the remarkable features of the doctrinal system of this psalm is the clear recognition it gives of the necessity, for the cleansing of the life, of the constant presence and activity of the Holy Spirit. "Take not Thy Holy Spirit from me and uphold me with a spirit of willingness." Thine to lead, mine to follow. Not autonomy but obedience, the ideal of the religious life. The operations of the Holy Spirit in the sphere of the moral life, the ethical activities of the Spirit, His sanctifying work, are but little adverted to in the Old Testament, and when alluded to, it is chiefly in promises for the Messianic period. Here, David not merely prays for them in his own case, but announces them as part of the experience of the past and present. His chance of standing, he says in effect, hangs on the continued presence of the Holy Spirit of God in him; in the upholding within him thereby of a spirit of willingness.

Thus we perceive that in its conception of God, of sin, of salvation alike, this psalm stands out as attaining the high-water mark of Old Testament revelation. It was by a hard pathway that David came to know God and himself so intimately. But he came thus to know both his own heart and the God of grace with a fullness and profundity of apprehension that it will be hard to parallel elsewhere. And it was no merely external knowledge that he acquired thus. It was the knowledge of experience. David knew sin because he had touched the unclean thing and sounded the depths of iniquity. He knew himself because he had gone his own way and had learned through what thickets and morasses that pathway led, and what was its end. And he knew God, because he had tasted and seen that the Lord is gracious. Yes, David had tasted and seen God's preciousness. David had experience of salvation. He knew what salvation was, and He knew its joy. But never had he known the joy of salvation as he knew it after he had lost it. And it is just here that the special poignancy of David's repentance comes in: it was not the repentance of a sinner merely; it was the repentance of a sinning saint.

It is only the saint who knows what sin is, for only the saint knows it in contrast with salvation, experienced and understood. And it is only the sinning saint who knows what salvation is, for it is only the joy that is lost and then found again that is fully understood. The depths of David's knowledge, the poignancy of his conceptions— of God, and sin, and salvation— carrying him far beyond the natural plane of his time and the development of the religious consciousness of Israel, may be accounted for, it would seem, by these facts. He who had known the salvation of God and basked in its joy, came to know through his dreadful sin what sin is, and its terrible entail; and through this horrible experience, to know what the joy of salvation is— the joy which he had lost and only through the goodness of God could hope to have restored. In the biting pain of his remorse, it all becomes clear to him. His sinful nature is revealed to him; and the goodness of God; his need of the Spirit; the joy of acceptance with God; the delight of abiding with Him in His house. Hence his profound disgust at himself; his passionate longing for that purity without which he could not see God. And hence his culminating prayer: "Restore unto me the joy of Thy salvation."

2

THE CONVICTION OF THE SPIRIT

John 16:8-11— "And He, when He is come, will convict the world in respect of sin, and of righteousness, and of judgment: of sin, because they believe not on Me; of righteousness, because I go to the Father, and ye behold Me no more; of judgment, because the prince of this world hath been judged."

These chapters which contain the closing discourse of Christ to His disciples are wonderingly dwelt upon by every Christian heart as the deepest and richest part of the riches of this Gospel. That we may obtain an insight into the marvelous words which we take as the subject of our meditation today, it is essential for us to realize the setting which our Lord gave them in the midst of this discourse. He had described to His disciples the conditions of their life, in continuous union and communion with Him, purchased as they were by His death for them and elevated to the lofty position of His special friends from whom He withholds nothing— not even His life itself. Then He had opposed to this picture of their exaltation, a delineation of their condition in the world, opposed and hated and persecuted and slain; while they, on their part, were to bear quietly their witness, endure their martyrdom, and trust in their Redeemer. But was this all? Were they condemned to a hopeless witness-bearing through all the coming years, while the world triumphed over them and in them over their crucified Lord? What an end to the hope they had cherished that this was He who should redeem Israel!

No, says the Lord, not the world, but they, were to win the victory; the laurel belongs by right not to Satan's but to His own brow. But we will not fail to notice the air of reproof with which He opens the section of His discourse which He has consecrated to an exposition of the victory over the world which He intended that they— as His— should win. "But now," He says, "I am going to Him that sent Me, and no one of you asketh Me, 'Whither goest Thou?', but because I said these things to you, sorrow hath filled your hearts." They had, indeed, expected Him to redeem Israel. It was therefore that they had given Him their trust, their love; that they had left their all to follow Him. But now sad days had come; and they saw their trusted Lord on the eve of giving Himself up to death. Was not this a dashing of their hopes? And had they, then, been so long time with Him and had not learned that the Father had ten myriad of angels who were encamped about Him and who would bear up His every footfall lest by chance He might dash His foot against a stone? Nay, that He had Himself power to lay down His life and to take it again? How could they look upon this coming death as an interference with His plans, the destruction of their hopes, and so sorrow as those without hope, instead of rejoicing as those who see the bright promise of the coming day in the east?

On the lines of these needs of the babes with which He had to deal, our Lord disposes His comforting words. The sorrow of their hearts He deprecates, not merely because He might expect them to rejoice like friends in His approaching departure to the higher and better life, but because He might expect them, after so much that He had done in their sight and spoken in their hearing, to have confidence in His mission and work, and to know that the power of Satan could not prevail against Him. What a spectacle we see here! The Master girding Himself for His last stroke of battle with the joy of victory in His eyes, while His surrounding friends are with streaming tears anointing Him for burial! He plants His foot firmly upon the steps of His Eternal Throne; and they smite their breasts with the sorrowful cry, "We had hoped that Thou mightest have been He that should have redeemed Israel! " No wonder that He gives them the loving rebuke, "But now I go My way to Him that sent Me,"— to Him that sent Me; on the completion of His work, then; not as balked, defeated, — " and no one of you asketh Me, 'Whither goest Thou?,' but because I have said these things sorrow hath filled your hearts."

Note how our Lord presses forward His personality here. "But I tell you the truth"— none of you has asked me, but I lovingly volunteer to tell you— "It is good for you that I go away." This departure is not a forced one, by way of defeat and loss; it was planned from the beginning and is part of the great plan by which I am to redeem not only Israel but the world. Note the emphatic "I": "It is good for you that I go away." Why this emphasis? Because there is another to whom this work has been committed and whose offices are necessary for the consummation of the work. "Because unless I go, the Helper will not come to you; but if I go, I will send Him to you; and it is He who, on His coming, will convict the world as to sin, and as to righteousness and as to judgment."

Let us observe: *First,* that Christ proclaims the victory. *Second,* that He announces the Agent through whose holy offices the victory will be realized in the world. *Third,* that He describes the manner in which the victory will be realized— by convicting the world. *Fourth,* that He names the three elements in which this conviction takes effect— sin, righteousness and judgment. And finally, *fifth,* that He points out the means which the Spirit uses to bring home this conviction, in each element, to the hearts of men.

Christ, I say, proclaims here the victory. Why are ye fearful, O ye of little faith? He says in effect to His tearful disciples. I go to the Father, and the world will hate you as it hated Me, and the world will persecute you and the world will slay you. But still the world is conquered. It is not because Satan is victor that I go to the Father; it is because I have completed My work, because redemption has been won, and I go to take My place upon the throne, that from that throne I may cause all things to work together for your good— that from it I may send the Helper forth to you, who will convict the world.

Here He announces the agent through whom the victory is to be realized in the world. He has won the victory; the Spirit is to apply His work that the fruits of the victory may be reaped to the full. A new age has dawned on this sin-stricken world; the prince of the power of the air is dethroned; the Prince of Peace reigns. Henceforth men strive not single-handed against the spiritual hosts of wickedness in high places; they have a Comforter, Advocate, Helper, Paraclete ever at their right hand, and He will give them the victory. It will be observed that Christ is here dealing with His apostles, not merely as individuals striving against the sin that is within them, but as His lieutenants, leading His hosts against the sin that is in the world. The world may persecute them— and slay them. But they will win the victory; by the power of their Helper, they will lead captivity captive.

Hence the nature of the victory that is to be realized in the world is here declared for us. It is a moral victory, a spiritual victory, and its essence is not physical subjection but mental and moral conviction. That Christ dies, that His followers are imprisoned, persecuted, slain, in no wise detracts from the victory; these things are disparate to it; they move on different planes and cannot convict. What the Helper is to do is to convict the world; and in this conviction rests their victory.

It is easy to see that this was a hard saying. No doubt when it was spoken, it fell like a deeper knell on the hearts of the apostles; instead of comforting, it pained; instead of encouraging, it slew. But then, Christ was not yet risen, and their eyes were restrained that they should know neither Him nor His victory. But turn to Pentecost. Then the Spirit came as He was promised and gave the convicting power to Peter's sermon that here was announced. See the joy in the victory, the exulting courage of the apostles, from that day to the end. Paul declares that he spoke not in the wisdom of the world but in the demonstration of the Spirit and in power. Although he uses a different word, what he means by the demonstration of the Spirit seems to be what Christ here promised under the name of the proof, convincing conviction of the Spirit. This phrase of Paul's, indeed, is perhaps the best verbal commentary on our passage. The best actual commentary is found, doubtless, in the narrative of the results of the apostolic preaching in the Book of' Acts. This, then, is the victory; not an external one over men's bodies, but the conquest of the world to Christ by the demonstration of the Spirit in the proclamation of the Gospel, whereby the world is convicted of sin and righteousness and judgment. The conquest is a spiritual one; the apostles are the agents in it; but the source of the power is the Holy Spirit— our one and true Helper in the world, who convicts the world of sin and righteousness and judgment.

We approach now the center of our subject and perceive what it is that the world is convicted of by the demonstration of the Spirit. The Savior pointedly discriminates between the three elements: as to sin, as to righteousness, as to judgment. Conviction of the world is the work of the Holy Spirit. Conviction as to what? (1) As to sin. The world, which as yet knows not sin, is convicted of it as the first and primary work of the Holy Spirit. It is not without significance that this is placed first. There is a sense in which it underlies all else, and conviction of sin becomes the first step in that recovery of the world, which is the victory. Once convicted of sin, another conviction is opened out before it. (2) It may then be convicted of righteousness, that is, of what righteousness is and what is required to form a true righteousness, and (3) it may be convicted of judgment, that is, of what judgment is, what justice requires and its inevitableness. These two together form the correlates of sin. It is only by knowing sin that we can know righteousness, as it is only by knowing darkness that we know light. We must know what sin is and how subtle it is before we can realize what righteousness is. We must know how base the one is before we can know how noble the other is. We must know the depth that we may appreciate the heights. In like manner, we must know sin in order to know judgment. We must know sin in its native hideousness that we may understand its ill-desert, and perceive with what judgment the sinner must be judged. So, too, we must know righteousness to know judgment. Not only the depths of sin, but also the heights of righteousness are involved in the judgment. Sin on the one side, righteousness on the other; these give us our true conviction of judgment. And the work of the Holy Spirit in the world is declared to be conviction; and by convicting men, He conquers the world. The Gospel is preached and it everywhere brings a crisis to men. Shall they hear or forbear? Some hear; to some it is hid; but on all the conviction takes effect. Sin is made known; righteousness is revealed; judgment is laid bare. And men convicted of their sin have but a choice of the righteousness or judgment.

For our Savior does not leave us in ignorance of the import and instruments of this threefold conviction:

(1) "Of sin," He says, "because they believe not on Me." This does not seem to mean that there would be no sin save for rejection of Christ, but that the proclamation of Christ is the great revealer of sin, the great distinguisher of men. When Christ is preached, the touchstone is applied, and men are convicted of being sinners and of the depths and hideousness of their sin by their exhibited attitude toward the Son of God. The Gospel is never hid save to them whose eyes the god of this world has blinded, lest they should see the glory of the Savior and come to Him and be saved. There is no revelation of character so accurate, so powerful, so unmistakable, so inevitable, as that wrapped up in the simple question, "What think ye of Christ?" Like a lodestone passing over a rubbish heap, His preaching draws to His side all that is not hopelessly bad. And all who come not are demonstrated to be sinners, and the depth of their sin is thus revealed.

(2) "As to righteousness," He adds, "because I go to My Father and ye see Me no more." This seems to mean that the fact of Christ's completed work, closed by His ascension to His primal glory, is the demonstration of righteousness. Convicted of sin, the world is also convicted of righteousness; that is, of the need of a righteousness such as it cannot frame for itself, and such as will match in its height the depth of its own sin. This is brought to light only in the Gospel, in which a righteousness of God is revealed from faith to faith. The convicting of the Holy Spirit consists no more of a conviction of human sinfulness and need of salvation than it does of the perfect righteousness of Christ wrought out on earth and sealed and warranted by His triumphal departure from this world. Men are convicted of sin because of their unbelief in Christ; of righteousness because of His finished work.

(3) But there is one more step. "As to judgment, because the prince of this world has been judged." If there is a sin and a righteousness, there is also a judgment. And men must know it. The third element in the Spirit's demonstration is the conviction of men of the overhanging judgment. This He performs by means of the obvious condemnation in Christ's person and work of the prince of this world, involving those who hold of his part in the same destruction. That the world and all that is in it is of the evil one, that there is no life in it and no help for the children of men, is one element of

the Spirit's testimony to the preached Gospel; that this world is under condemnation and reserved for the eternal fire is but another element of it. Everywhere where the Spirit carries His demonstration men know what judgment is, and they know it by perceiving the judgment of the evil one.

We should not permit to slip from our minds that we have here the Savior's own exposition of the method and manner of His spiritual conquest of the world. This conquest is assured. It is the Spirit who performs it. And the method of His work in it is by accompanying the preached word with His demonstration and power. This demonstration of the Spirit consists in convicting the world of sin, of righteousness, and of judgment. Is conviction of sin then, we may ask, necessary to salvation? Is conviction of sin the first step of salvation? Let those smitten souls at Pentecost answer, who cried aloud, "Men and brethren, what shall we do?" Is conviction of righteousness necessary to salvation? A convinced and convicted appreciation of the needs of our soul which alone can be found in Christ Jesus? Ask him who has proved to us that the whole world lies alike under the wrath of God, and that by the works of the law no flesh can be justified, and who adds to this word of terror the only word of hope: "But now apart from the law a righteousness of God has been revealed, even the righteousness of God through faith in Jesus Christ, unto all them that believe; for there is no difference, for all have sinned and fallen short of the glory of God" (Romans 3:21-23). And as to conviction of judgment, ask Felix, who trembled as this same Paul reasoned of righteousness and temperance and judgment to come.

Assuredly, my brethren, would we be saved, we must know what sin is, we must know what righteousness is and where it may be found, and we must tremble before the judgment which that righteousness must pass on our sin. Christ has performed His work, and with the shout of "It is finished" upon His lips, has ascended to His throne on high, and there, seated by the right hand of God, He has shed forth this which we even now see and hear. The Spirit is in the world and wherever the Gospel of God's grace is faithfully preached, He attends it with His demonstration and power. And what does He demonstrate to our souls? That we are sinners; that we need a God-provided righteousness; that otherwise we must partake in the judgment of the prince of this world. This is God's way and it is the only way. Let us be fully assured of it!

3

THE OUTPOURING
OF THE SPIRIT

Acts 2:16,17a— "This is that which hath been spoken through the prophet Joel ... I will pour forth of My Spirit."

In any attempt to estimate the significance of the outpouring of the Spirit at Pentecost, considered as the inauguration of the New Dispensation, the following two considerations must be made fundamental.

The Spirit was active under the Old Dispensation in all the modes of His activity under the New Dispensation. This is evinced by the records of the activities of the Spirit of God in the Old Testament, which run through the whole series of the Spirit's works, and by the ascription by the writers of the New Testament of all the working of the Spirit of God in the Old Testament to their own personal Holy Spirit. Thus, for example, the inspiration of the Old Testament prophets and writers is ascribed to the Holy Spirit (2 Pet. 1:21; 1 Pet. 1:11; Heb. 3:7; 10:15; Matt. 22:43; Mark 12:36; Acts 1:16; 28:25). The authorship of the ritual service of the sanctuary is ascribed to Him (Heb. 9:8). The leading of Israel in the wilderness and throughout its history is ascribed to Him (Acts 7:51). It was in Him that Christ preached to the antediluvians (1 Pet. 3:18,19). He was the author of faith then as now (2 Cor. 4:13).

Nevertheless, the change of dispensation consisted primarily just in this: that in the New Dispensation the Spirit was given (John 7:39; 16:7; 20:22; Acts 2).

The problem, therefore, is to understand how the New Dispensation can be thus, by way of discrimination, the Dispensation of the Spirit, characterized by the giving of the Spirit, while yet He was active in the Old Dispensation in all the modes of His activity under the New. For the solving of this problem we shall need to exercise a humble courage in embracing the standpoint of Scripture itself.

In order to do this, we must observe that the operations of the Holy Spirit were forfeited by man through sin. Adam enjoyed the influence of the Holy Spirit, and it was through the Spirit's inworking that Adam was enabled to withstand temptation, and by it that he might have been led safely through his probation and afterwards confirmed in holiness. When Adam sinned, he lost the gift of original righteousness, indeed, but with it also the gift of the Holy Spirit, and the depravation into which he and his posterity sank — according to the fearful history recorded in the first chapter of Romans — has lying at its foundation the deprivation of the Holy Spirit's influences.

The Lord never, indeed, wholly turns away from any work of His hands; did He do so, it would fall at once on the removal of His upholding hand, like the unhooped barrel, back into nothingness. In His providence, and in what we call His common grace, He continues to work among even His sinful creatures who have lost all claim upon His love. But just because they are sinful, they have forfeited all the operations of His grace and deserve at His hands only wrath. After the sin of Adam, the whole world lies in wickedness; and just because it lies in wickedness, it is deprived of the inhabitation of the Spirit of holiness.

But though the race has thus by its sin forfeited the right to the inward work of the Holy Spirit, God may in His infinite grace restore the Spirit to man, as soon as, and insofar as, He can make it just and righteous so to do. In the atoning work of Christ, He has laid the foundation for such a restoration in righteousness. But we are dependent on the Scriptures to inform us how far this restoration extends intensively and extensively. We are not authorized to argue that because of the remedy for sin offered in Christ, God must or may treat sin as if it never had existed, so that all that the race has lost in Adam is restored in Christ, and that for all the sinful race alike. It may be consonant with what we could wish to be true, so to argue. But it is obvious that were this, in fact, the state of the case, the race would have been restored in Christ from the moment of Adam's fall, and would have been continued in unbroken holy development. Adam's sin would, in that case, have been a benefit to the race; it would have curtailed its probation and placed the race at once at the goal of attainment which had been promised to obedience. Obedience and disobedience obviously would, in that case, have been all one; the end obtained would have been precisely the same. Whence it would follow that Adam's probation was a mere farce, if not even that the divine regard for moral distinctions was a pretense.

Nothing can be more obvious according to either Scripture or the experience of the race than that this course was not taken. The Lord did not, at once, treat sin as if it had never occurred. He did, indeed, at once institute a remedial scheme by which the effect of sin might be obliterated to the extent and in the manner which was pleasing to His glorious judgment; but clearly it was not pleasing to Him, on the basis of the atonement, to set aside the fact of sin altogether. How far, on this basis, He was pleased to set aside the fact of sin and restore to men the Spirit of holiness of whom they had been deprived on account of sin, we are wholly dependent upon His Word to tell us.

On the basis of the Scriptural declarations, it is perfectly evident that it was not the plan of God to restore the lost Spirit to man universally. The dreadful fact stares us full in the face that God has thought well to leave some men eternally without the Spirit of holiness. It is obvious that in the execution of His plan of discrimination among men, it was not His plan to distribute the saving operations of His Spirit equally through either space or time. His sovereignty shows itself not only in passing by one individual and granting His grace to another, but also in passing by one nation, or one age, and granting His grace to another. And in His inscrutable wisdom it has obviously been His plan to confine the operations of His grace through many ages to one people of His choice, passing by the nations of the world at large and leaving them to their sin. This is the meaning of the choice of Israel and the divine guidance of that chosen people.

We cannot fathom all the purpose of God in this disposition of His grace. We may see directly, however, that thus a twofold end was secured. Sin was allowed to work itself out on the stage of a worldwide life, with the result that it exhibited all its horror and all its helplessness. And grace continuously had its trophies on the stage of Israelitish life. Israel thus served as a foil to exhibit the corruption of the nations, and at the same time preserved the continuity of God's people through time and supplied the starting point for the universal extension of His Kingdom when at length the set time for its inauguration should come. At all events, it is a fact that the Scriptures, on which we are dependent for all knowledge of the work of God's Spirit, confine all their declarations of the work of the Spirit through these gathering years to the theocratic people. Only within and for the benefit of the theocracy does the Spirit of God work from Adam to Christ— from the first man through whom came death to the Second Man through whom came redemption.

And now we are, perhaps, in a position to understand the contrast between the first and second dispensations, when the second is called the Dispensation of the Spirit, inaugurated by the visible outpouring of the Spirit at Pentecost, although the Spirit had been the Guide of Israel, and the Sanctifier of the people of God from the beginning. The new dispensation is the Dispensation of the Spirit, whether we consider the extent of the Spirit's operations, the object of His operations, the mode of the divine administration of His Kingdom, or the intensity of the Spirit's action.

The new dispensation is the Dispensation of the Spirit because in it the Spirit of God is poured out upon all flesh. This element in the change is made emphatic in the predictions which prepared the way for it— as in the prophecy of Joel which Peter quotes in his Pentecostal sermon; and it is symbolized in the miraculous attestation by which it is inaugurated— in the tongues that distributed themselves on the heads of the agents of the new proclamation— "as if of fire"— and in the "gift of tongues" by which the universality of their mission was intimated. Here is the central idea of the new dispensation. It is worldwide in its scope; the period of preparation being over, the worldwide Kingdom of God was now to be inaugurated, and the Spirit was now to be poured upon all flesh. No longer was one people to be its sole recipients, but the remedy was to be applied to all peoples alike.

The new dispensation is the Dispensation of the Spirit, again, because now the object of the Spirit's work is, for the first time, to recover the world from its sin. Of course, this was its ultimate object from the beginning; but during the period preparation, it was only its ultimate, not its proximate object. Its proximate object then was preparation, now it was performance. Then it was to preserve a seed, sound and pure for the planting; now it was the reaping of the harvest. It required the Spirit's power to keep the seed safe during the cold and dark winter; it requires it now to plant the seed and water it and cause it to grow into the great tree, in the branches of which all the fowls of the air may rest. The Spirit is the leaven which leavens the world; in Israel it is that leaven laid away in the closet until the day of leavening comes; when that day comes and it is drawn out of its dark corner and placed in the heap of meal— then, indeed, the day of the leaven has come. Or to use a figure of Isaiah's, during all those dark ages the Kingdom of God, confined to Israel, was like a pent-in stream. The Spirit of God was its life, its principle, during all the ages; it was He that kept it pent-in. Now the Kingdom of God is like that pent-in stream with the barriers broken down and the Spirit of God driving it.

The new dispensation is, once more, the Dispensation of the Spirit, because now the mode of the administration of God's Kingdom has become spiritual. This is in accordance with its new extent and its new object, and is intended to secure and to advance its universality and its rapid progress. In the old dispensation, the Kingdom of God was, in a sense, of *this* world; it had its relation to and its place among earthly states; it was administered by outward ordinances and enactments and hierarchies. In the new dispensation, the Kingdom of God is not of this world; it has no relation to or place among earthly states; it is not administered by external ordinances. The Kingdom of God now is within you; its law is written on the heart; it is administered by an inward force. Where the Jewish ordinances extended, there of old was the Kingdom of God; where men were circumcised on the eighth day, where they turned their faces to the Temple at the hours of sacrifice, and whence they went up to Jerusalem to the annual feasts. A centralized worship we say, for the Temple at Jerusalem was the place where God might be acceptably worshipped, and they were of the Kingdom who owned its sway. Now, "where the Spirit of the Lord is, there is the Church"— as Tertullian and Irenaeus and Ignatius tell us; wherever the Spirit works— and He works when and where and how He will— there is the Church of God. We are freed from the outward ordinances, such as, touch not, taste not, handle not, and are under the sway of the indwelling Spirit alone. An inward power takes the place of an outward commandment; love shed abroad in our hearts supplants fear as our motive; a divine strength replaces our human weakness.

Finally, we may say that the new dispensation is the Dispensation of the Spirit, because now the Spirit works in the hearts of God's people with a more prevailing and a more pervading force. We cannot doubt that He regenerated and sanctified the souls of God's saints in the old dispensation; we cannot doubt that He was operating creatively in them in renewing their hearts, and that He was powerfully present in them, leading them in right paths. "Create within me a new heart and renew a right spirit within me" is an Old Testament prayer, and it must represent an Old Testament experience. And yet we seem to be not merely authorized but compelled to look upon the mode of the Spirit's work as more powerful and prevailing in the new dispensation than in the old. For in these new times, God seems to promise not only that He will pour out His Spirit upon all flesh, but that He will pour Him out in an especial manner on His people. In what sense would the fact that He will pour out the Spirit on the seed of Israel be characteristic of the new dispensation, if there were not some advance here on the old. Such a passage as Ezekiel 36:26 or Zechariah 12:10 would seem to mean as much as this: that the Holy Spirit will work so powerfully in the hearts of God's people in the new time, that the sanctification which had lagged behind in the old should be completed now. That is to say, there is here the promise of a holy Church. This too, no doubt, is of progressive realization. After a number of Christian centuries, we have cause still to weep over the backslidings of the people of God as truly as Israel had. But Christ is perfecting His Church even as He perfects the individual, and after a while He will present it to Himself a holy Church, without spot or wrinkle or any such thing.

Surely it must mean much to us that we live in the dispensation of the Spirit, a dispensation in which the Spirit of God is poured out upon all flesh with the end of extending the bounds of God's Kingdom until it covers the earth; and that He is poured out in the hearts of His people so that He reigns in their hearts and powerfully determines them to do holiness and righteousness all the days of their lives. Because we live under this dispensation, we are free from the outward pressure of law and have love shed abroad in our hearts, and, being led by the Spirit of God, are His sons, yielding a willing obedience and by instinct doing what is conformable to His will. Because this is the Dispensation of the Spirit, we are in the hands of the loving Spirit of God whose work in us cannot fail; and the world is in His powerful guidance and shall roll on in a steady development until it knows the Lord and His will is done on earth as in heaven. It is because this is the Dispensation of the Spirit that it is a missionary age; and it is because it is the Dispensation of the Spirit that missions shall make their triumphant progress until earth passes at last into heaven. It is because this is the Dispensation of the Spirit that it is an age of ever-increasing righteousness, and it is because it is the Dispensation of the Spirit that this righteousness shall wax and wax until it is perfect. Blessed be God that He has given it to our eyes to see this His glory in the process of its coming.

4

THE LEADING
OF THE SPIRIT

Romans 8:14 — "For as many as are led by the Spirit of God, these are the sons of God."

These words constitute the classical passage in the New Testament on the great subject of "the leading of the Holy Spirit." They stand, indeed, almost without strict parallel in the New Testament. We read, no doubt, in that great discourse of our Lord's which John has preserved for us, in which, as He was about to leave His disciples, He comforts their hearts with the promise of the Spirit, that "when He, the Spirit of truth, is come, He shall guide you into all the truth" (John 16:13). But this "guidance into truth" by the Holy Spirit is something very different from the "leading of the Spirit" spoken of in our present text; and it is appropriately expressed by a different term. We read also in Luke's account of our Lord's temptation that He was "led by the Spirit in the wilderness during forty days, being tempted by the devil," (Luke 4:1,2) where our own term *is* used. But though undoubtedly this passage throws light upon the mode of the Spirit's operation described in our text, it can scarcely be looked upon as a parallel passage to it. The only other passage, indeed, which speaks distinctly of the "leading of the Spirit" in the same sense of our text is Galatians 5:18, where in a context very closely similar, Paul again employs the same phrase: "But if you are led by the Spirit, you are not under the law." It is from these two passages primarily that we must obtain our conception of what the Scriptures mean by "the leading of the Holy Spirit."

The Holy Spirit

There is certainly abundant reason why we should seek to learn what the Scriptures mean by "spiritual leading." There are few subjects so intimately related to the Christian life, of which Christians appear to have formed, in general, conceptions so inadequate, where they are not even positively erroneous. The sober-minded seem often to look upon it as a mystery into which it would be well not to inquire too closely. And we can scarcely expect those who are not gifted with sobriety to guide us in such a manner into the pure truth of God. The consequence is that the very phrase, "the leading of the Spirit," has come to bear, to many, a flavor of fanaticism. Many of the best Christians would shrink with something like distaste from affirming themselves to be "led by the Spirit of God" and would receive with suspicion such an averment on the part of others as indicatory of an unbalanced religious mind. It is one of the saddest effects of extravagance in spiritual claims that, in reaction from them, the simple-minded people of God are often deterred from entering into their privileges. It is surely enough, however, to recall us to a careful searching of Scripture in order to learn what it is to be "led by the Spirit of God," simply to read the solemn words of our text: "As many as are led by the Spirit of God, these are the sons of God." If the case be so, surely it behooves all who would fain believe themselves to be God's children to know what the leading of the Spirit is.

Let us, then, commit ourselves to the teaching of Paul, and seek to learn from him what is the meaning of this high privilege. And may the Spirit of Truth here, too, be with us and guide us into the truth.

Approaching the text in this serious mood, the first thing that strikes us is that the leading of the Spirit of God of which it speaks is not something peculiar to eminent saints, but something common to all God's children, the universal possession of the people of God.

"As many as are led by the Spirit of God," says the Apostle, "these are the sons of God." We have here, in effect, a definition of the sons of God. The primary purpose of the sentence is not, indeed, to give this definition. But the statement is so framed as to equate its two members, and even to throw a stress upon the co-extensiveness of the two designations. "As many as are led by the Spirit of God, these

32

and these only are the sons of God." Thus, the leading of the Spirit is presented as the very characteristic of the children of God. This is what differentiates them from all others. All who are led by the Spirit of God are thereby constituted the sons of God; and none can claim the high title of sons of God who are not led by the Spirit of God. The leading of the Spirit thus appears as the constitutive fact of sonship. And we dare not deny that we are led by God's Spirit lest we therewith repudiate our part in the hopes of a Christian life. In this aspect of it, our text is the exact parallel of the immediately preceding declaration, which it thus takes up and repeats: "Now if anyone does not have the Spirit of Christ, he is not His" (Rom. 8:9).

It is obviously a mistake, therefore, to look upon the claim to be led by God's Spirit as an evidence of spiritual pride. It is rather a mark of spiritual humility. This leading of the Spirit is not some peculiar gift reserved for special sanctity and granted as the reward of high merit alone. It is the *common* gift poured out on *all* God's children to meet their *common* need, and it is the evidence, therefore, of their *common* weakness and their *common* unworthiness. It is not the reward of special spiritual attainment; it is the condition of *all* spiritual attainment. In its absence we would remain hopelessly the children of the devil; by its presence alone are we constituted the children of God. It is only because of the Spirit of God shed abroad in our hearts that we are able to cry, "Abba, Father" (Rom. 8:15).

We observe, therefore, next, that the end in view in the spiritual leading of which Paul speaks is not to enable us to escape the difficulties, dangers, trials, or sufferings of this life, but specifically to enable us to conquer sin.

Had the former been its object, it might indeed have been a special grace granted to a select few of God's children, and its possession might have separated them from among their brethren as the peculiar favorites of the Deity. Since, however, the latter is its object, it is the appropriate gift of all those who are sinners, and it is the condition of their conquest over the least of their sins. In the preceding context, Paul discloses to us our inherent sin in all its festering rottenness. But he discloses to us also the Spirit of God as dwelling in us and forming the principle of a new life. It is by the presence of the Spirit within us alone that the bondage in which we are by nature held to sin is broken, that we are emancipated from sin and are no longer debtors to live according to the flesh. This new principle of life reveals itself in our consciousness as a power claiming regulative influence over our actions, leading us, in a word, into holiness.

If we consider our life of new obedience from the point of view of our own activities, we may speak of ourselves as fighting the good fight of faith; a deeper view reveals it as the work of God in us by His Spirit. When we consider this divine work within our souls with reference to the end of the whole process, we call it *sanctification;* when we consider it with reference to the process itself, as we struggle on day by day in the somewhat devious and always thorny pathway of life, we call it *spiritual leading.* Thus the "leading of the Holy Spirit" is revealed to us as simply a synonym for sanctification when looked at from the point of view of the pathway itself, through which we are led by the Spirit as we more and more advance toward that conformity to the image of His Son, which God has placed before us as our great goal.

It is obvious at once then how grossly it is misconceived when it is looked upon as a peculiar guidance granted by God to His eminent servants in order to insure their worldly safety, worldly comfort, even worldly profit. The leading of the Holy Spirit is always for good; but it is not for all goods, but specifically for spiritual and eternal good. I do not say that the good man may not, by virtue of his very goodness, be saved from many of the sufferings of this life and from many of the failures of this life. How many of the evils and trials of life are rooted in specific sins we can never know. How often even failure in business may be traced directly to lack of business integrity rather than to pressure of circumstances or business incompetency is mercifully hidden from us. Nor do I say that the gracious Lord has no care for the secular life of His people. But it surely is obvious that the leading of the Spirit spoken of in the text is not in order to guide men into secular goods; and it is not to be inferred to be absent when trials come— sufferings, losses, despair of this world. It is specifically in order to guide them into eternal good, to make them not prosperous, not free from care or suffering, but holy, free from sin. It is not given us to preserve us from the necessity of strenuous preparation for the tasks before us or from the trouble of rendering decision in the difficult crises of life. It is given specifically to save us from sinning, to lead us in the paths of holiness and truth.

Accordingly, we observe next that the spiritual leading of which Paul speaks is not something sporadic, given only on occasion of some special need of supernatural direction, but something continuous, affecting all the operations of a Christian man's activities throughout every moment of his life.

It has but one end in view, the saving from sin, the leading into holiness, but it affects every single activity of every kind— physical, intellectual, and spiritual— bending it toward that end. Were it directed toward other ends, we might indeed expect it to be more sporadic. Were it simply the omniscience of God placed at the disposal of His favorites, which they might avail themselves of in times of perplexity and doubt, it might well be occasional and temporary. But since it is nothing other than the power of God unto salvation, it must needs abide with the sinner, work constantly upon him, enter into all his acts, condition all his doings, and lead him thus steadily onward toward the one great goal.

It is easy to estimate, then, what a perversion it is of the "leading of the Spirit" when this great saving energy of God, working continually in the sinner, is forgotten, and the name is accorded to some fancied sporadic supernatural direction in the common offices of life. Let us not forget, indeed, the reality of providential guidance, or imagine that God's greatness makes Him careless of the least concerns of His children. But let us much more not forget that the great evil under which we are suffering is sin, and that the great promise which has been given us is that we shall not be left to wander, self-directed, in the paths of sin into which our feet have strayed, but that the Spirit of holiness shall dwell within us, breaking our bondage and leading us into that other pathway of good works, which God has prepared beforehand that we should walk in them.

All of this will be powerfully supported and the subject perhaps somewhat further elucidated if we seek now to penetrate a little deeper into the inmost nature of the work of the Holy Spirit, which Paul calls here a "leading," by attending more closely to the term which he has chosen to designate it when he calls it by this name. This term, as those skilled in such things tell us, is one which throws emphasis on three matters: first, on the extraneousness of the influence under which the movement suggested takes place; second, on the completeness of the control which this influence exerts over the action of the subject led; and third, on the pathway over which the resultant progress is made. Let us glance at each of these matters in turn.

One is not led when he goes his own way. It is only when an influence distinct from ourselves determines our movements that we can properly be said to be led. When Paul, therefore, declares that the sons of God are "led by the Spirit of God," he emphasizes, first of all, the distinction between the leading Spirit and the led sons of God. As much as this he declares with great emphasis, that there is a power within us, not ourselves, that makes for righteousness. And he identifies this extraneous power with the Spirit of God. The whole preceding context accentuates this distinction, inasmuch as its entire drift is to paint the conflict which is going on within us between our native impulses which make for sin, and the intruded power which makes for righteousness. Before all else, then, spiritual leading consists in an influence over our actions of a power which is not to be identified with ourselves— either as by nature or as renewed— but which is declared by the apostle Paul to be none other than the Spirit of God Himself.

We thoroughly misconceive it, therefore, if we think of spiritual leading as only a conquest of our lower impulses by our higher nature, or even as a conquest by our regenerated nature of the remnants of the old man lingering in our members. Both of these conquests are realities of the Christian life. The child of God will never be content to be the slave of his lower impulses, but will ever strive, and with ultimate success, to live on the plane of his higher endowments. The regenerated soul will never abide the remnants of sin that vex his members, but will have no rest until he eradicates them to the last shred. But these victories of our nobler selves— natural or gracious— over what is unworthy within us do not so much constitute the essence of spiritual leading as they are to be counted among its fruits. Spiritual leading itself is not a leading of ourselves by ourselves, but a leading of us by the Holy Spirit. The declaration of its reality is the declaration of the reality of the indwelling of the Holy

Spirit in the heart, and of the subjection of the activities of the Christian heart and life to the control of this extraneous power. He that is led by the Spirit of God is not led by himself or by any element of his own nature, native or acquired, but is led by the Holy Spirit. He has ceased to be what the Scriptures call a "natural man," and has become what they call a "spiritual man"; that is, to translate these accurately, he has ceased to be a self-led man and has become a Spirit-led man— a man led and determined in all his activities by the Holy Spirit. It is this extraneousness of the source of these activities which Paul emphasizes first of all when he declares that the sons of God are led by the Spirit of God.

The second matter which is emphasized by his declaration is the controlling power of the influence exerted on the activities of God's children by the Holy Spirit. One is not led, in the sense of our text, when he is merely directed in the way he should go, guided, as we may say, by one who points out the path and leads only by going before in it; or when he is merely upheld while he himself finds or directs himself to the goal.

The Greek language possesses words which precisely express these ideas, but the Apostle passes over these and selects a term which expresses *determining control over our actions*. Some of these other terms are used elsewhere in the Scriptures to set forth appropriate actions of the Spirit with reference to the people of God. For example, our Lord promised His disciples that when the Spirit of Truth would come, He would *guide* them into all the truth (John 16:13). Here a term is employed which does not express controlling leading, but what we may perhaps call *suggestive leading*. It is used frequently in the Greek Old Testament of God's guidance of His people, and once, at least, of the Holy Spirit: "Teach us to do Thy will, for Thou art my God; let Thy good Spirit guide us in the land of uprightness" (Ps. 143:10). But the term which Paul employs in our text is a much stronger one than this. It is not the proper word to use for a guide who goes before and shows the way, or even of a commanding general, say, who leads an army. It has stamped upon it rather the conception of the exertion of a power of control over the actions of its subject, which the strength of the led one is insufficient to withstand.

This is the proper word to use, for example, when speaking of leading animals, as when our Lord sent His disciples to find the donkey and her colt and commanded them "to loose them and *lead* them to Him" (Matt. 21:2); or as when Isaiah declares in the Scripture which was being read by the eunuch of Ethiopia, whom Philip was sent to meet in the desert, "He was *led* as a sheep to the slaughter" (Acts 8:32; cf. Isa. 53:7). It is applied to the conveying of sick folk— as men who are not in a condition to control their own movements; as, for example, when the good Samaritan set the wounded traveler on his own beast and led him to an inn and took care of him (Luke 10:34); or when Christ commanded the blind man of Jericho "to be led unto Him" (Luke 18:40). It is most commonly used of the enforced movements of prisoners; as when we are told that they led Jesus to Caiaphas to the place (John 18:28); or when we are told that they seized Stephen and led him into the council (Acts 6:12); or that Paul was provided with letters to Damascus unto the synagogues, "that if he found any that were of the Way, he might lead them bound to Jerusalem" (Acts 9:2). In word, though, the term may, of course, sometimes be used when the idea of force retires somewhat into the background, and is commonly so used when it is transferred from external compulsion to internal influence— as, for example, when we are told that Barnabas took Paul and led him to the apostles (Acts 9:2), and that Andrew led Simon unto Jesus (John 1:42)— yet the proper meaning of the word includes the idea of control, and the implication of prevailing determination of action never wholly leaves it.

Its use by Paul on the present occasion must be held, therefore, to emphasize the controlling influence which the Holy Spirit exercises over the activities of the children of God in His leading of them. That extraneous power which has come into our hearts making for righteousness, has not come into them merely to suggest to us what we should do— merely to point out to us from within the way in which we ought to walk— merely to rouse within us and keep before our minds certain considerations and inducements toward righteousness. It has come within us to take the helm and to direct the motion of our frail barks on the troubled sea of life. It has taken hold of us as a man seizes the halter of an ox to lead it in the way which he would have it go; as an attendant conducts the sick in leading him to the physician; as the jailer grasps the prisoner to lead him to trial or to the jail. We were slaves to sin; a new power has entered into us to break that bondage— but not that we should be set, rudderless, adrift on the ocean of life, but that we should be powerfully directed on a better course, leading to a better harbor.

Accordingly Paul, when he declares that we have been emancipated from the law of sin and of death by the advent of the law of the Spirit of life in Christ Jesus into our hearts, does not leave it so, as if emancipation were all. He adds, "Accordingly then, we are bound." Though emancipated, still bound! We are bound, but no longer to the flesh, to live after the flesh, but to the Spirit, to live after the Spirit. He hastens, indeed, to point out that this is no hard bondage, but a happy one; that sons is a name better fitted to express its circumstances than "slaves"— that it includes childship and heirship to God and with Christ. But all this blessed assurance operates to exhibit the happy estate of the service into which we have been brought, rather than to alter the nature of it as service. The essence of the new relation is that it also is one of control, though a control by a beneficent and not a cruel power. We do not at all catch Paul's meaning, therefore, unless we perceive the strong emphasis which lies on this fact— that those who are led by the Spirit of God are under the control of the Spirit of God. The extraneous power which has come into us, making for righteousness, comes as a controlling power. The children of God are not the directors of their own activities; there is One that dwells in them who is not merely their guide, but their governor and strong regulator. They go, not where they would, but where He would; they do not what they might wish, but what He determines. This it is to be led by the Spirit of God.

It is to be observed, however, on the other hand, that although Paul uses a term here which emphasizes the controlling influence of the Spirit of God over the activities of God's children, he does not represent the action of the Spirit as a substitute for their activities. If one is not led, in the sense of our text, when he is merely guided, it is equally true that one is not led when he is carried. The animal that is led by the attendant, the blind man that is led to Christ, the prisoner that is led to jail— each is indeed under the control of his leader, who alone determines the goal and the pathway, but each also proceeds on that pathway and to that goal by virtue of his own powers of locomotion.

There was a word lying at the Apostle's hand by which he could have expressed the idea that God's children are borne by the Spirit's power to their appointed goal of holiness, apart from any activities of their own, had He elected to do so. It is employed by Peter when he would inform us how God gave His message of old to His prophets. "For no prophecy," he tells us, "ever came by the will of man: but men spake from God, being borne by the Holy Spirit" (2 Peter 1:21). This term, "borne," emphasizes, as its fundamental thought, the fact that all the power productive of the motion suggested is inherent in, and belongs entirely to, the mover. Had Paul intended to say that God's children are taken up, as it were, in the Spirit's arms and borne, without effort on their own part, to their destined goal, he would have used this word. That he has passed over it and made use of the word "led" instead indicates that, in his teaching, the Holy Spirit leads and does not carry God's children to their destined goal of holiness; that while the Spirit determines both the end and the way toward it, His will controlling their action, yet it is by their effort that they advance to the determined end.

Here, therefore, there emerges an interesting indication of the difference between the Spirit's action in dealing with the prophet of God in imparting through him God's message to men, and the action of the same Spirit in dealing with the children of God in bringing them into their proper holiness of life. The prophet is "borne" of the Spirit; the child of God is "led." The prophet's attitude in receiving a revelation from God is passive, purely receptive; he has no part in it, adds nothing to it, is only the organ through which the Spirit delivers it to men; he is taken up by the Spirit, as it were, and borne along by Him by virtue of the power that resides in the Spirit, which is natural to Him, and which, in its exercise, supersedes the natural activities of the man. Such is the import of the term used by Peter to express it. On the other hand, the son of God is not purely passive in the hands of the sanctifying Spirit; he is not borne, but led— that is, his own efforts enter into the progress made under the controlling direction of the Spirit; he supplies, in fact, the force exerted in attaining the progress, while yet the controlling Spirit supplies the entire directing impulse. Such is the import of the term used by Paul to express it. Therefore, no prophet could be exhorted to work out his own message with fear and trembling; it is not left to him to work it out— the Holy Spirit works it out for him and communicates it in all its rich completeness to and through him. But the children of God are exhorted to work out their own salvation in fear and trembling because they know the Spirit is working in them both the willing and the doing according to His own good pleasure.

In order to appreciate this element of the Apostle's teaching at its full value, it is perhaps worthwhile to observe still further that in his choice of a term to express the nature of the Spirit's action in leading God's children, the Apostle avoids all terms which would attribute to the Spirit the power employed in making progress along the chosen road. Not only does he not represent us as being carried by the Spirit; he does not even declare that we are drawn by Him. There was a term in common use which the Apostle could have used had he intended to express the idea that the Spirit drags, by physical force as it were, the children of God onward in the direction in which He would have them go. This term is actually used when the Savior declares that no man can come unto Him except the Father draw him (John 6:44)— which is as much as to say that men in the first instance do not and cannot come to Christ by virtue of any powers native to themselves, but require the action upon them of a power from without coming to them, drawing their inert, passive weight to Christ, if they are to be brought to Him at all. We can identify this act of drawing— "dragging" would perhaps express the sense of the Greek term none too strongly— with that act which we call, in our theological analysis, regeneration, and which we explain in accordance with the import of this term, as the monergistic act of God, impinging on a sinner who is and remains, as far as this act is concerned, purely passive, and therefore does not move, but is moved.

Such, however, is not the method of the Spirit's leading of which Paul speaks in our text. This is not a drawing or dragging of a passive weight toward a goal which is attained, if attained at all, only by virtue of the power residing in the moving Spirit, but a leading of an active agent to an end determined indeed by the Spirit, and along a course which is marked out by the Spirit, but over which the soul is carried by virtue of its own power of action and through its own strenuous efforts. If we are not borne by the Spirit out of our sin into holiness with a smooth and easy movement, almost unnoticed by us or noted only with the languid pleasure with which a child resting peacefully on its mother's breast may note its progress up some rough mountain road, so neither are we dragged by the Spirit as a passive weight over the steep and rugged path. We are led. We are under His control and walk in the path in which He sets our feet. It is His part to keep us in the path and to bring us at length to the goal. But it is we who tread every step of the way; our limbs that grow weary with the labor; our hearts that faint; our courage that fails— our faith that revives our sinking strength, our hope that instills new courage into our souls— as we toil on over the steep ascent.

And thus it is most natural that the third matter to which Paul's declaration that we are led by the Spirit of God directs our attention concerns the pathway over which our progress is made.

One is not led who is unconscious of the road over which he advances; such a one is rather carried. He who is led treads the road himself, is aware of its roughness and its steepness, pants with the effort which he expends, is appalled by the prospect of the difficulties that open out before him, rejoices in the progress made, and is filled with exultant hope as each danger and obstacle is safely surmounted. He who is led is in the hands of an extraneous power, of a power which controls his actions, but the pathway over which he is thus led is trodden by his own efforts— by his own struggles it may be — and the goal that is attained is attained at the cost of his own labor.

When Paul chooses this particular term, therefore, and declares that the sons of God are led by the Spirit, he is in no way forgetful of the arduous nature of the road over which they are to advance, or of the strenuous exertion on their own part by which alone they may accomplish it. He strengthens and comforts them with the assurance that they are not to tread the path alone, but he does not lull them into inertness by suggesting that they are not to tread it. The term he employs avouches to them the constant and continuous presence with them of the leading Spirit, not merely setting them in the right path, but keeping them in it and leading them through it; for it designates not an impulse which merely initiates a movement in a given direction, but a continuous, unbroken influence determining a movement to its very goal. But his language does not promise them relief from the weariness of the journey, alleviation of the roughness of the road, freedom from difficulty or danger in its course, or emancipation from the labor of travel. That they have been places in the right path, that they will be kept continuously in it, that they will attain the goal— of this he assures them; for this it is to be led of the Spirit of God, a power not ourselves controlling our actions, prevalently directing our movement to an end of His choice. But He does not encourage us to relax our own endeavors; for he who is led, even though it be by the Spirit of God, advances by virtue of his own powers and his own efforts. In a word, Paul chooses language to express the action of the Spirit on the sons of God which is in perfect harmony with his exhortation to the children of God to which we have already alluded— to work out their own salvation with fear and trembling because they know it is God that is working in them both the willing and the doing according to His own good pleasure.

What a strong consolation for us is found in this gracious assurance— poor, weak children of men as we are! To our frightened ears, the text may come at first as with the solemnity of a warning: "As many as are led by the Spirit of God, these and these only are sons of God." Is there not a declaration here that we are not God's children unless we are led by God's Spirit? Knowing ourselves, and contemplating the course of our lives and the character of our ambitions, dare we claim to be led by the Spirit of God? Is this life— this life that I am living in the flesh— is this the product of the Spirit's leading? Shall not despair close in upon me as I pass the dreadful judgment on myself that I am not led by God's Spirit, and that I am, therefore, not one of His sons? Let us hasten to remind ourselves, then, that such is not the purport nor the purpose of the text. It stands here not in order to drive us to despair, because we see we have sin within us, but to kindle within us a great fire of hope and confidence because we perceive we have the Holy Spirit within us.

Paul, as we have seen, does not forget the sin within us. Who has painted it and its baleful power with more vigorous touch? But neither would he have us forget that we have the Holy Spirit within us, and what that blessed fact, above all blessed facts, means. He would not have us reason that because sin is in us, we cannot be God's children; but in happy contradiction to this, that because the Holy

Spirit is in us, we cannot but be God's children. Sin is great and powerful; it is too great and too powerful for us; but the Holy Spirit is greater and more powerful than even sin. The discovery of sin in us might bring us to despair did not Paul discern the Holy Spirit in us— who is greater than sin— that he may quicken our hope.

This declaration that frightens us is not written, then, to frighten, but to console and to enhearten. It stands here for the express purpose of comforting those who would despair at the sight of their sin. Is there a conflict of sin and holiness in you? asks Paul. This very fact that there is conflict in you is the charter of your salvation. Where the Holy Spirit is not, there conflict is not; sin rules undisputed lord over the life. That there is conflict in you, that you do not rest in complacency in your sin, is a proof that the Spirit of God is within you, leading you to holiness. And all who are led by the Spirit of God are the children of God; and if children, then heirs, heirs of God and joint heirs with Christ Jesus. This is the purport of the message of the text to us. Paul points us not to the victory of good over evil, but to the conflict of good with evil— not to the end but to the process— as the proof of childship to God. The note of the passage is, thus, not one of fear and despair, but one of hope and triumph. "If God be for us, who can be against us?"— that is the query the Apostle would have ring in our hearts. Sin has a dreadful grasp upon us; we have no power to withstand it. But there enters our hearts a power not ourselves making for righteousness. This power is the Spirit of the most high God. "If God be for us who can be against us?" Let our hearts repeat this cry of victory today.

And as we repeat it, let us go onward, in hope and triumph, in our holy efforts. Let our slack knees be strengthened and new vigor enter our every nerve. The victory is assured. The Holy Spirit within us cannot fail us. The way may be rough; the path may climb the dizzy ascent with a rapidity too great for our faltering feet; dangers, pitfalls are on every side. But the Holy Spirit is leading us. Surely, in that assurance, despite dangers and weakness, and panting chest and swimming head, we can find strength to go ever forward.

In these days, when the gloom of doubt, if not even the blackness of despair, has settled down on so many souls, there is surely profit and strength in the certainty that there is a portal of such glory before us and in the assurance that our feet shall press its threshold at the last. In this assurance we shall no longer beat our disheartened way through life in dumb despondency and find expression for our passionate but hopeless longings only in the wail of the dreary poet of pessimism:

> "But if from boundless spaces no answering voice shall start,
> Except the barren echo of our ever yearning heart—
> Farewell, then, empty deserts, where beat our aimless wings,
> Farewell, then, dream sublime of uncompassable things."

We are not, indeed, relieved from the necessity for healthful effort, but we can no longer speak of "vain hopes." The way may be hard, but we can no longer talk of "the unfruitful road which bruises our naked feet." Strenuous endeavor may be required of us, but we can no longer feel that we are "beating aimless wings" and can expect no further response from the infinite expanse than "a sterile echo of our own eternal longings." No, no— the language of despair falls at once from off our souls. Henceforth, our accents will be borrowed rather from a nobler "poet of faith," and the blessing of Asher (Deut. 33:25-27) will seem to be spoken to us also:

> "Thy shoes shall be iron and brass,
> And as thy days, so shall thy strength be.
> There is none like unto God, O Jeshurun,
> Who rideth upon the heavens for thy help,
> And in His excellency on the skies.
> The eternal God is thy dwelling place,
> And underneath are the everlasting arms."

5

THE SPIRIT'S TESTIMONY TO OUR SONSHIP

Romans 8:16 — "The Spirit Himself bears witness with our spirit that we are children of God."

"The Spirit Himself bears witness with our spirit that we are children of God." This is one of the texts of the Bible to which the Christian heart turns with especial longing and to which it clings with especial delight. On it has been erected the great Protestant doctrine of assurance— the great doctrine that every Christian man may and should be assured that He is a child of God— that it is possible for him to attain this assurance and that to seek and find it is accordingly his duty. So much as that it certainly, along with kindred texts, does establish. The Holy Spirit Himself, it affirms, bears witness with our spirit that we are children of God; and then it goes on to develop the idea of childship to God from the point of view of the benefits it contains: "and if children then heirs, heirs of God and joint heirs with Christ."

It is quite obvious that the object of the whole is to encourage and enhearten; to speak, in a word, to the Christian's soul a great word of confidence. We are not to be left in doubt and gloom as to our Christian hope and standing. A witness is adduced and this no less a witness than the Holy Spirit, the Author of all truth. We are not committed to our own tentative conjectures or to our own imaginations and fancies. The Holy Spirit bears co-witness with our spirit that we are God's children. Surely, here there is firm standing ground for the most timid feet.

No wonder that men have seized hold of such an assurance with avidity, and sought and found in it peace from troubled consciences and hesitating fears. No wonder either if they have sometimes, in their eagerness for a sure foundation for their hope, pressed a shade beyond the mark and sought on the basis of this text an assurance from the Holy Spirit for a fact of which they had no other evidence, if, indeed, they did not feel that they had evidence enough against it; an assurance conveyed, moreover, in a mode that would be independent of all other evidence, if, indeed, it did not bear down and set aside abundant evidence to the contrary. This occasional use of the text to ground an assurance which seems to the observer unjustified, if not positively negated by all appearances, has naturally created a certain amount of hesitation in appealing to it at all or in seeking to attain the gracious state of assurance which it promises. This is a most unprofitable state of affairs. And in its presence among us, no less than in the presence of a somewhat exaggerated appeal to the testimony of the Spirit, we may find the best of warrants for seeking to understand just what the text affirms and just what privileges it holds out to us.

And here, first, the text leaves no room for doubt that the testimony of the Holy Spirit that we are God's children is a great reality. This is not a matter of inference from the text; it is expressed by it in *totidem verbis*[3]. Exactly what is affirmed is that "the Spirit Himself bears witness with our spirit that we are children of God." The actuality of the Spirit's testimony to our childship to God is established, then, beyond all cavil; it is entrenched in the same indeclinable authority by which we are assured that there is a Spirit at all, that there is any such thing as an adoption into sonship to God, or that it is possible for sinful mortals to receive that adoption— the authority of the inspired Word of God. That the Spirit witnesses with or to our spirits that we are children of God is just as certain, then, as that there is such a state as sonship to which we may be introduced or that there is such a being as the Spirit of God to bear witness of it. These great facts all stand or fall together. And that is as much as to say that no Christian man can doubt the fact of the testimony of the Spirit that we are children of God. It is accredited to him by the same authority which accredits all that enters into the very essence of Christianity. It is, in fact, one of the elements of a full system of Christian truth that must be acknowledged by all who accept the system of Christian truth.

It would seem to be equally clear from the text that the testimony of the Spirit is not to be confounded with the testimony of our own consciousness. However the text be read, the "Spirit of God" and "our spirit" are brought into pointed contrast in it and are emphatically distinguished from one another. Accordingly, not only does H. A. W. Meyer, who understands the text of the joint testimony of the divine and human spirits, say: "Paul distinguishes from the subjective self-consciousness, I am the child of God, the therewith accordant testimony of the objective Holy Spirit, Thou art the child of God"; but Henry Alford also, who understands the text to speak solely of the testimony of the Spirit, borne not with but to our spirit, remarks: "All are agreed, and indeed the verse is decisive for it, that it is something separate from and higher than all subjective conclusions"— language which seems, indeed, scarcely exact, but which is certainly to the present point. It is of no importance for this whether Paul says that the Spirit bears witness with or to our spirit; in either case, he distinctly distinguishes the Spirit of God from our spirit along with which or to which He bears His witness. And not only so, but this distinction is the very nerve of the whole statement, the scope of which is nothing other than to give the Christian, along with his human conclusions, also a divine witness.

Not only, then, is the distinction, here emphatically instituted, available, as Meyer reminds us, as a clear *dictum probans*[4] against all pantheistic confusion of the divine and human spirits in general, and all mystical confusion and inter-smelting of the divine and human spirits in the Christian man, as if the regenerated spirit was something more than a human spirit, or was in some way interpenetrated and divinitized by the divine Spirit, but it is equally decisive against identifying out-of-hand the testimony of the Spirit of God here spoken of with the testimony of our own consciousness. These are different things, not only distinguishable but to be distinguished. The witness of the Holy Spirit is something other than, additional to, and more than the witness of our own spirit; and it is adduced here just because it is something other than, additional to, and more than the witness of our own spirit. The whole sense of Paul's declaration is that we have, over and beyond our own authority, a Divine witness to our childship to God on which we may rest without fear that we shall be put to shame.

It is to be borne in mind, however, that distinctness in the source of this testimony from that of our own consciousness is not the same as separateness from it in its delivery. Paul would seem, indeed, while thus strongly emphasizing its distinct source— namely, the Divine Spirit— nevertheless to suggest its conjunction with the testimony of our own spirit in its actual delivery. This, indeed, he would seem frankly to assert, if, as seems most natural, we are to understand the preposition in the phrase, "bears testimony with," to refer to our spirit and are to translate with our English version, "The Spirit Himself bears witness with our spirit." So taken, the conjunction is as emphatic as the distinction. It must not be overlooked, however, that some commentators prefer to take "our spirit" as the object to which the testimony is borne: "the Spirit bears witness to our spirit"— in which case the emphasis on the conjunction of the testimony of the Spirit of God with that of our spirit may be lost. I say, may be lost; for even then the preposition in the verb will need to be accounted for; and it would seem to be still best to account for it by referring it to our spirit— "the Spirit Himself bears its consentient witness to our spirit," His witness consenting to our spirit's witness. And I say merely that the emphasis on the conjunction may be lost; for even if this interpretation be rejected and the force of the preposition be found merely in the accordance of the witness with the fact, by which it is the truth and trustworthiness of the testimony alone which is emphasized, nevertheless the connection of the verse with the preceding one is still implicative of the conjoined witness of the two spirits. For it is in our crying, "Abba, Father," that the witness of the Spirit of God is here primarily found— the relation of this verse to the preceding being practically the same as if it were expressed in the genitive absolute[5]— thus: "the Spirit which we received was the Spirit of adoption whereby we cry, "Abba, Father,"— the Spirit Himself testifying thus to our spirit that we are children of God."

The fact that the conjunction of the two witnesses thus dominates the passage, however its special terms are explained, adds a powerful

reason for following the natural interpretation of the terms themselves and referring the preposition "with" directly to the "our spirit."
It is with considerable confidence, therefore, that we may understand
Paul to say that "the Spirit Himself bears witness together with our
spirit that we are children of God," and thus not merely to imply or
assert— as in any case is the fact— but pointedly to emphasize the
conjunction, or, if you will, the confluence of the divine testimony
with that of the human consciousness itself. Distinct in its source, it
is yet delivered confluently with the testimony of our human consciousness. To be distinguished from it as something other than, additional to, and more than the testimony of our human consciousness, it is yet not to be separated from it as delivered apart from it,
out of connection with it, much less in opposition contradiction to it.
"The Spirit of God," says that brilliant young thinker whose powers
were the wonder, as well as the dependence, of the Westminster Divines, "is not simply a martyr— a witness— but co-martyr— *qui simul
testimonium dicit* — He bears witness not only to but with our spirit,
that is, with our conscience. So that if the witness of our conscience
be blank, and can testify nothing of sincerity, hatred of sin, love to
the brethren, or the like, then the Spirit of God witnesses no peace
or comfort to that soul; and the voice that speaks peace to a person
who has no gracious mark or qualification in him, does not speak
according to the Word, but contrary to the Word, and is, therefore, a
spirit of delusion." "So that in the business of assurance and full persuasion, the evidence of graces and the testimony of the Spirit are
two concurrent causes or helps, both of them necessary. Without the
evidence of graces, it is not a safe nor a well-grounded assurance;
without the testimony of the Spirit, it is not a *plerophory* or full assurance." And then he devoutly adds: "Therefore, let no man divide the
things which God has joined together."

These remarks of George Gillespie's will already suggest to us the
function of this testimony of the Holy Spirit as set forth by Paul as a
co-testimony with the witness of our own spirit. It is not intended as
a substitute for the testimony of our spirit or, to be more precise, of
"signs and marks"— but as an enhancement of it. Its object is not to
assure a. man who has "no signs" that he is a child of God, but to
assure him who has "signs," but is too timid to draw so great an inference from so small a premise, that he is a child of God and to give

him thus not merely a human but a divine basis for his assurance. It is, in a word, not a substitute for the proper evidence of our childship, but a divine enhancement of the evidence. A man who has none of the marks of a Christian is not entitled to believe himself to be a Christian; only those who are being led by the Spirit of God are children of God. But a man who has all the marks of being a Christian may fall short of his privilege of assurance. It is to such that the witness of the Spirit is superadded, not to take the place of evidence of "signs," but to enhance their effect and raise it to a higher plane; not to produce an irrational, unjustified conviction, but to produce a higher and more stable conviction than he would be, all unaided, able to draw; not to supply the lack of evidence, but to cure a disease of the mind which will not profit fully by the evidence.

We are here in the presence of a question which has divided the suffrages of Christian men from the beginning. The controversy has raged in every age, whether our assurance of our salvation is to be syllogistically determined thus: the promise of God is sure to those who believe and obey the Gospel; I believe and obey the Gospel; hence I am a child of God: or is rather to be mystically determined by the witness of the Holy Spirit in the heart; whether we are to examine ourselves for signs that we are in the faith, or, neglecting all signs, are to depend on the immediate whisper of the Spirit to our heart, "You are a child of God." The debate has been as fruitless as it has been endless. And the reason is that it is founded on a false antithesis, and, being founded on a false antithesis, each side has had something of truth to which it was justified in clinging in the face of all refutation, and something of error which afforded an easy mark for the arrows of its opponents. The victory can never be with those who contend that we must depend for our assurance wholly on the marks and signs of true faith; for true assurance can never arise in the heart save by the immediate witness of the Holy Spirit, and he who looks not for that can never go beyond a probable hope of being in Christ. The victory can never be with those who counsel us to neglect all signs and depend on the testimony of the Holy Spirit alone; for the Holy Spirit does not deliver His testimony save through and in confluence with the testimony of our own consciences that we are God's children. "All your marks," says Gillespie with point, "will leave you in the dark if the Spirit of Grace does not open your eyes so that you may know the things which are freely given to you of God"; and again with equal point, "To make no trials by marks and to trust an inward testimony, under the notion of the Holy Spirit's testimony, when it is without the least evidence of any true gracious mark . . . is a deluding and an ensnaring of the conscience."

It is obvious that the really cardinal question here, therefore, concerns not the fact of the testimony of the Holy Spirit, not its value or even its necessity for the forming of a true assurance, but the mode of its delivery. It is important, therefore, to interrogate our text upon this point. The single verse before us does not speak very decisively to the matter; only by its conjunction of the testimony of the Spirit with that of our own spirit does it suggest an answer. But nowhere than in these more recondite doctrines is it more necessary to read our texts in their contexts; and the setting of our text is very far from being without a message to us in these premises. For how does Paul introduce this great assertion? As already remarked, as practically a subordinate clause to the preceding verse, with the virtual effect of a genitive absolute.[5] He had painted in the seventh chapter the dreadful conflict between indwelling sin and the intruded principle of holiness which springs up in every Christian's breast. And he had pointed to the very fact of this conflict as a banner of hope. For he identifies the fact of the conflict with the presence of the Holy Spirit working in the soul; and in the presence of the Holy Spirit is the earnest of victory. The Spirit would not be found in a soul which was not purchased for God and in process of fitting for the heavenly kingdom. Let no one talk of living on the low plane of the seventh chapter of Romans. Low plane, indeed! It is a low plane where there is no conflict. Where there is conflict— with the Spirit of God as one party in the battle - there is progressive advance towards the perfection of the Christian life. So Paul treats it. He points to the conflict as indicative of the presence of the Spirit; he points to the presence of the Spirit as the earnest of victory; and on this experience he founds his promise of eternal bliss. Then comes our passage, introduced with one of his tremendous "therefores." "Accordingly, then, brethren,"— since the Holy Spirit is in you and the end is sure,— "accordingly, then, we are debtors not to the flesh to live after the flesh, but to the Spirit to live after the Spirit . . . For as many as are being led" (notice the progressive present) "by the Spirit of God, there are sons of God, for" (after all) "the spirit that ye received was not a spirit of bondage, but a spirit of adoption, whereby we cry Abba Father,— the Spirit Himself bearing witness with our spirit that we are children of God." "The Spirit Himself" bearing this witness? When? How? Why, of course, in this very cry framed by Him in our souls, "Abba, Father!" Not a separate witness; but just this witness and no other. The witness of the Spirit, then, is to be found in His hidden ministrations by which the filial spirit is created in our hearts, and comes to birth in this joyful cry.

We must not fancy, however, that, therefore, the witness of the Spirit adds nothing to the syllogistic way of concluding that we are children of God. It does not add another way of reaching this conclusion, but it does add strength of conclusion to this way. The Spirit is the spirit of truth and will not witness that he is a child of God who is not one. But he who really is a child of God will necessarily possess marks and signs of being so. The Spirit makes all these marks and signs valid and available for a true conclusion— and leads the heart and the mind to this true conclusion. He does not operate by producing conviction without reason; an unreasonable conclusion. Nor yet apart from the reason; equally unreasonable. Nor by producing more reasons for the conclusion. But by giving their true weight and validity to the reasons which exist and so leading to the true conclusion, with Divine assurance. The function of the witness of the Spirit of God is, therefore, to give to our halting conclusions the weight of His Divine certitude.

It may be our reasoning by which the conclusion is reached. It is the testimony of the Spirit which gives to a conclusion thus reached indefectible certainty. It is the Spirit alone who is the Author, therefore, of the Christian's firm assurance. We have grounds, good grounds, for believing that we are in Christ, apart from His witness. Through His witness these good grounds produce their full effect in our mind and hearts.

6

THE SPIRIT'S HELP
IN OUR PRAYING

Romans 8:26, 27— "Likewise the Spirit also helps in our weakness. For we do not know what we should pray for as we ought; but the Spirit Himself makes intercession for us with groanings which cannot be uttered. Now He who searches the hearts knows what the mind of the Spirit is, because He makes intercession for the saints according to the will of God."

The direct teaching of this passage obviously is that the Holy Spirit, dwelling in Christian men, indites their petitions, and thus secures for them both that they shall ask God for what they really need and that they shall obtain what they ask. There is here asserted both an effect of the Spirit's working on the heart of the believer and an effect of this, His working on God. Even Christian men are full of weakness, and neither know what they should pray for in each time of need, nor are able to pray for it with the fervidness of desire which God would have them use. It is by the operation of the Spirit of God on their hearts that they are thus led to pray aright in matter and manner, and that their petitions are rendered acceptable to God, as being according to His will. This is the obvious teaching of the passage; but that we may fully understand it in its implications and shades, it will be desirable to look at it in its context.

The Holy Spirit

The eighth chapter of Romans is an outburst of humble triumph on the Apostle's part, on realizing that the conflict of the Christian life as depicted in the seventh chapter issues in victory, through the indwelling of the Holy Spirit. Evil may be entrenched in our members, but the power of God unto salvation has entered our hearts by the Holy Spirit, and by the prevalent working of that Holy Spirit in us, we are enabled to cry, "Abba, Father," and being made sons of God, are constituted His heirs and coheirs with Jesus Christ. Not as if, indeed, we are to be borne without effort of our own into this glorious inheritance "to be carried to the skies on flowery beds of ease." No! "Surely we must fight, if we would win." For, after all, the Christian life is a pilgrimage to be endured, a journey to be accomplished, a fight to be won. Least of all men was the Apostle Paul, whose life was in labors more abundant and in trials above measure, liable to forget this. It is out of the experiences of his own life as well as out of the nature of the thing that he adds, therefore, to his cry of triumph a warning of the nature of the life which, nevertheless, we must still live in the flesh. If "the Spirit Himself beareth witness with our spirits that we are the sons of God," and the glorious sequence follows, " and if children, then heirs, heirs of God and joint heirs with Christ," no less do we need to be reminded further of the condition underlying the victory— "if so be that we suffer with Him that we may also be glorified with Him." To share with Christ His glory implies sharing with Him His sufferings. "Must Jesus tread the path alone and all the world go free?" Union with Him implies taking part in all His life experiences, and we can ascend the throne with Him only by treading with Him the pathway by which He ascended the throne. It was from the cross that He rose to heaven.

The rest of this marvelous chapter seems to be devoted to encouraging the saint in his struggles as he treads the thorny path with Christ. The first encouragement is drawn from the relative greatness of the sufferings here and the glory yonder; the second, from the assistance in the journey received from the Holy Spirit; and the third, from the gracious oversight of God over the whole progress of the journey. This whole section of the chapter, therefore, appears as Paul's word of encouragement to the believer as he struggles on in his pilgrimage— in his "Pilgrim's Progress"— in view of the hardships, and sufferings and trials attendant in this sinful world on the life in Christ. It is substantially, therefore, an Apostolic commentary on our Lord's words, "If any man would come after Me, let him deny himself and take up his cross and follow Me;" "he that doth not take up his cross and follow after Me, is not worthy of Me." These sufferings, says Paul, are inevitable; no cross, no crown. But he would strengthen us in enduring the cross by keeping on the crown, by assuring us of the presence of the Holy Spirit as our ever-present Helper and by reminding us of the divine direction of it all. Thus he would alleviate the trials of the journey.

Our text then takes its place as one of these encouragements to steadfast constancy, endurance, in the Christian life— to what we call today "perseverance." The "weakness," "infirmity," to which it refers is to be taken, therefore, in the broadest sense. No doubt its primary reference may be to the remnant of indwelling sin, not yet eradicated and the source of all the Christian's weaknesses. But it is not confined to this. It includes all that comes to a Christian as he suffers with Christ, all that is included in our Lord's requirement of denying ourselves and taking up our cross. Paul's life of suffering for the Gospel's sake may be taken by us, as it, doubtless, was felt by him as he penned these words, as an illustration of the breadth of the meaning of the word. He who would live godly must in every age suffer a species of persecution; a species differing in kind with the tone and temper and quality of each age, but always persecution. He who would follow after Christ must meet with many opposers. A strenuous life is the Christian life in the world; it is appropriately designated a warfare, a fight. But we are weak. And the weakness meant is inclusive of all human weaknesses in the stress of the great battle.

The encouragement which Paul offers us in this our confessed weakness, is the ever-present aid of the Holy Spirit. We are not to be left to tread the path, to fight the fight, alone; the Spirit ever "helpeth" our weakness, "takes our burden on Himself, in our stead and yet along with us," as the double compound word expresses. He does not take it away from us and bear it wholly Himself, but comes to our aid in bearing it, receiving it also on His shoulders along with us. In giving this encouragement of the ever-present aid of the Spirit in our weakness, the Apostle adds an illustration of it. And it is exceedingly striking that, in seeking an illustration of it, the Apostle thinks at once of the sphere of prayer. It shows his estimate of the place of prayer in the Christian struggle, that in his eye, prayer is really "the Christian's vital breath." Our weakness, he seems to say, is helped primarily by the Spirit through His inditing our prayers for us. Perhaps this will not seem strange to us if we will fitly consider what the Christian life is in its dependence on God; and what prayer is, in its attitude of dependence on God. Prayer is, in a word, the correlate of religion. The prayerful attitude is the religious attitude. And that man is religious who habitually holds toward God, in life and thought, in act and word, the attitude of prayer. Is it not fitting, after all, that Paul should encourage the Christian man, striving to live a Christian life— denying himself and taking up his cross and following Christ— by assuring him primarily that the Holy Spirit is ever present, helping him in his weakness, to this effect that his attitude toward God, in his conscious dependence on Him, should be kept straight? For this it is to help us in prayer.

Nor can it seem strange to us that Paul adverts to our need of aid in prayer in the very matter of our petitions. It is worth noting how very vitally he writes here, doubtless again, out of his own experience. "We know not what we should pray for," he says, "in each time of need "— according, that is, to the needs of each occasion. It is not lack of purpose— it is lack of wisdom that he intimates. We may have every desire to serve God and every willingness to serve Him at our immediate expense, but do we know what we need at each moment? The wisest and best of men must needs fail here. So Paul found when he asked three times that the thorn in the flesh might be removed and halted not till the Lord had told him explicitly that His grace was sufficient for him. How often we would rather escape the suffering that lies in our path than receive of the grace of God! Nay, a greater than Paul may here be our example. Did not our Lord Himself say, "Now is my soul troubled; and what shall I say? Father, save Me from this hour." Quick, though, came the response back from His own soul, "But for this cause came I unto this hour: Father, glorify Thy name," yet may we not see even in this momentary hesitation a hint of that uncertainty of which all are more or less the prey? It is not merely in the recalcitrances of the Christian life— God knows we have need enough there!— but it is not only in the recalcitrances and the mere unwillingnesses of the Christian life that the Spirit aids us; but in the perplexities of the Christian life too. Under His leading we shall not only be saved from sins, but also from mistakes, in the will of God. And thus He leads us not only to pray, but to pray "according to the will of God."

And now, how does the Spirit thus aid us in praying according to the will of God? Paul calls it a making of intercession for us with groanings which cannot be uttered; making intercession for us or in addition to us, for the word could have either meaning. It is clear from the whole passage that this is not an objective intercession in our behalf— made in heaven as Christ our Mediator intercedes for us. That the Spirit makes intercession for us is known to God, not as God in heaven, but as "Searcher of hearts." It is equally clear that it is not an intercession through us as mere conduits, unengaged in the intercession ourselves; it is an intercession made by the Spirit as our Helper and not as our substitute. It is equally clear that it is not merely in our natural powers that the Spirit speaks; it is a groaning of which the Spirit is the Author and "over and above" our own praying. It is clear then that it is subjective and yet not to be confused with our own prayings. Due to the Spirit's working in our hearts, we conceive what we need in each hour of need and ask God for it with unutterable strength of desire. The Spirit intercedes for us then by working in us right desires for each time of need, and by deepening these desires into unutterable groans. They are our desires and our groans. But not apart from the Spirit. They are His, wrought in us by Him. And God, who searches the heart, sees these unutterable desires and "knows the mind of the Spirit that He is making intercession for the saints according to the will of God."

Thus, then, the Spirit helps our weakness. By His hidden, inner influences, He quickens us to the perception of our real need; He frames in us an infinite desire for this needed thing; He leads us to bring this desire in all its unutterable strength before God, who, seeing it within our hearts, cannot but grant it, as accordant with His will. Is not this a very present help in time of trouble? As prevalent a help as if we were miraculously rescued from any danger? And yet a help wrought through the means of God's own appointment, that is, our attitude of constant dependence on Him and our prayer to Him for His aid? And could Paul here have devised a better encouragement to the saints to go on in their holy course and fight the battle bravely to the end?

7

THE SPIRIT OF FAITH

2 Corinthians 4:13 — "But having the same Spirit of faith, according to that which is written, 'I believed, and therefore did I speak,' we also believe, and therefore also we speak."

This verse is a declaration on the Apostle's part of the grounds of his courage and faithfulness in preaching the glorious Gospel of Christ. The circumstances which attended his proclamation of this Gospel were of the most oppressive. In the preceding verses, we have a picture of them which is drawn by means of a series of declarations which rise, one after another, to a most trying climax. He says that in the prosecution of his work, he is in every way pressed, perplexed, pursued, smitten down. Here is a vivid picture of the defeated warrior, who is not only pressed by the foe, but put at his wits ends— not merely thus discouraged, but put to flight— not merely pursued, but smitten down to the earth. A lurid picture of the befallings of Paul as a minister of Christ amid the spiritual conflicts on this side and that, in Galatia and in Corinth! Nevertheless, things have not come to an end with him. Side by side with this series of befallings, he places a contrasting series which exhibits the marvelous continuance of the Apostle in his well-doing, in spite of such dreadful happenings to him. Though he is in every way pressed, yet he is not brought to his last straits; though he is in every way perplexed, yet he has not gone to despair; though he is pursued, yet he is not overtaken; though he is actually smitten down, he is yet not destroyed.

60

The Spirit of Faith

In the prosecution of Paul's work as a minister of Christ there is thus a marvelous coexistence of experiences the most desperate and of deliverances the most remarkable. It is as if destruction had continually befallen him; yet ever out of destruction he rises afresh to the continuance of his work. In this remarkable contrast of his experiences, the Apostle sees a dramatic reenactment of Christ's saving work, who died that He might live and might bring life to the world. In it he sees himself, he says, ever reenacting the putting to death of Jesus that the life also of Jesus may be manifested in his body. As Jesus died and rose again, so he daily dies in the service of Christ and comes to life again; and so, abiding in life, he is ever delivered to death for Jesus' sake that the life also of Jesus might be manifested in his mortal flesh. Oh, marvelous destiny of the followers of Christ in the very nature and circumstances of their service to placard before the world the great lesson of the redemption of Christ— the great lesson of life by death: to manifest thus to all men the life of Jesus and the life from Jesus springing constantly out of His death. Thus the very life circumstances of Paul become a preached Gospel. They manifest Christ and His work for souls. They manifest it. For the dying is for Paul and the life for his hearers.

Now Paul gives a twofold account of those circumstances in which he preached the Gospel. He assigns them ultimately to the purpose of God. This great treasure of the glorious Gospel has been put into such earthen vessels for the very purpose of more fully manifesting its divine glory. In contrast with its vehicle, the power of the message is all the more discernible. It is just that the exceeding greatness of its power may be seen to be of God, that it is delivered to men in vessels whose exceeding weakness may be apparent. On the other hand, that these earthen vessels are able to endure the strain put upon them in conveying these treasures is itself from God. Paul attributes it to God's upholding power operating through faith. That in the midst of such trials he is enabled to endure; that though smitten down continuously, he is not destroyed; that though dying daily, he still lives with a living Gospel still on his lips; it is all due to the support of his firm conviction and faith. "So then, it is death that worketh in us but life in you, and having the same Spirit of faith, according as it is written, I believed and, therefore, did I speak; we also believe and therefore speak, since we know that He that raised up Jesus shall raise us up

61

also with Jesus and shall present us with you." Here are the sources of the Apostle's strength and of his courage. It is only because of his firm faith in the Gospel he preaches that he can endure through the trials into which its service has immersed him. With a less clear conviction and less firm faith in it, he would long ago have succumbed to the evils of his life and his lips have long ago become dumb. But he believed; and, therefore, though earth and hell combined to destroy him, he could not but speak. Let earthly trials multiply; beyond the daily deaths of earth there was an eternal life in store for him; and the more he could rescue from death to that life, the more multiplied grace would redound to increased thanksgiving and abound to God's glory. In the power of this faith the Apostle can face and overcome the trials of life.

There are many important lessons that may come to us from observing this declaration of the Apostle's faith.

Beginning at the remoter side, we may be surprised to observe that he seeks the norm of his faith in the Old Testament saints. "Having the same Spirit of faith," he says, "according as it is written, I believed, and therefore did I speak"— referring for the model of faith back to the words of this hero Psalmist. Now we may not be accustomed to think of the Old Testament saints as the heroes of faith. The characteristic emotion of Old Testament religion, we are accustomed to say, was awe or even fear. The characteristic expression of it is summed up in the term, "the fear of the Lord." The New Testament, on the other hand, is the dispensation of faith. And if we have consideration only for the prevailing language of the Old Testament, this is true enough. The word "faith " is scarcely an Old Testament word; it occurs but twice in the English Old Testament, and it is disputable whether on either occasion it fairly— or at least fully— represents the Hebrew. Even the word "to believe" applied to divine things, is rare in the Old Testament.

But the word and the thing are different matters. And it may be doubted whether the conceptions of awe, fear, and of faith, trust, are so antagonistic as is commonly represented. Certainly reverence and faith are correlative conceptions. A God whom we do not fear with religious reverence, we cannot have such faith in as the Apostle's. And certainly the New Testament writers do always look to the Old Testament saints as the heroes of faith. This is the burden of one of the most magnificent passages in the New Testament, the eleventh chapter of Hebrews. And of others too. It is the faith of Abraham which is the standing model of faith to both Paul and James; and it is he who, both in the subjective and objective senses of the word, is represented to us as the Father of the Faithful. Let it be allowed that these heroes of faith lived in the twilight of knowledge; knowledge and faith stand in relation to one another, but are not the measure of one another. If there can be no faith where there is no knowledge, on the other hand, it is equally true that the realm of dim knowledge is often the region of strong faith— for when we walk by sight, faith has no place. No; he that believes in Jesus, whom he has seen, must yield, in point of heroism of faith and the blessedness promised to it, to him who, having not seen, yet has believed. Those great men of God of old, not being weak in faith, believed in the twilight of revelation, and waxing strong, died in faith; and we could wish nothing higher for ourselves than that we might be like them in their faithful faith.

It is observable next that the Apostle attributes the faith of the Old Testament heroes, to whom he would direct our eyes as the norm of faith, to the work of the Holy Spirit. He felicitates himself not merely on having the same quality of faith with them. He looks deeper. The ground of rejoicing in their fellowship is that he shares with them the "same Spirit of faith." "Having the same Spirit of faith," he says. It may be doubted, once again, if we should have naturally spoken in this way. We may be accustomed to think of the Holy Spirit as an essentially New Testament possession; and to conceive, in a more or less formulated manner, of the saints of the Old Testament as left to their own native powers in their serving of God. Heroes of faith as they were, it would be peculiarly difficult, however, to believe that they reached the height of their pious attainment apart from the gracious operations of the Spirit of God. Or shall we say that only in New Testament times men are dead in sin, and only in these days of the completed Gospel and of the New Covenant do men need the almighty power of God to raise them from their spiritual death?

Certainly the Bible lends no support to such a notion. Less is said of the gracious operations of the Spirit in the Old Testament than in the New, but to say less of it is one thing, and its absence is quite another. And there is enough in the Old Testament itself— by prayer of psalmist that the Holy Spirit should not be taken away from him, by statement of historian that through the Spirit, God gave this one and that one a new heart, by assurance of prophet that the Spirit of God is the Author of all right belief and of all good conduct— to assure us that then, too, on Him depended all the exercises of piety; to Him was due all the holy aspirations and all the good accomplishments of every saint of God. And certainly the New Testament tells us in repeated instances that the Holy Spirit was active throughout the period of the Old Dispensation in all the varieties of activities which characterize the New. The difference between the two lies not in any difference in the utter dependence of men on Him, or in the nature of His operations, but in their extent and aim with reference to the life of the Kingdom of God. Our present passage is one of those tolerably numerous New Testament ones in which the gracious operations of the Spirit in the Old Covenant are assumed. Paul here tells us that the faith of the Old Testament saints was the product of God's Holy Spirit; and he claims for himself nothing more than what he asserts for them. "Having the same Spirit of faith," he says. He is content— nay, he is full of joy— to have the same Spirit working faith in him that worked faith in them. He claims no superiority in the matter. If he has a like faith, it is because he is made by God's grace to share in a like fountain of faith. The one Spirit who works faith is the common possession of them and of him; and therein he finds his highest privilege and his greatest glory. What David had of the operations of the Spirit, that is what Paul represents as the height of Christian privilege to possess.

It may not be wholly needless to observe further the naturalness of Paul's ascription of faith to the working of the Holy Spirit— whether under the Old or the New Dispensation. He means to express the confidence he has in the glorious Gospel which he proclaims. He does not say, however, simply "having a confident faith." He says, "having the Spirit of faith," the same Spirit of faith which wrought in the Psalmist. So much was faith to him the product of the Spirit that he thinks of it in terms of its origin. Clearly to him, no Spirit, no faith. Faith is, therefore, most absolutely conceived by the Apostle as the product not of our own powers, but of the Spirit of God, and it is inconceivable to him that it can exist apart from His gift.

We may sometimes fall short of the Apostle's conception and fancy that we can— nay, that we must first believe before the Spirit comes to us. No, it is the Spirit who gives faith. Faith is the gift of God in its innermost essence; and the Apostle continually thanks God for it as His gift. We find it enumerated in Galatians 5:23 among the fruits of the Spirit; in 1 Corinthians 12:7, we find it among the gifts which the Spirit distributes to men. In our present passage, it is emphasized as the work of the Spirit, by its being used as a characterizing description of the Spirit. We do not describe or define a thing by something which is common to it and others. The possession of a vertebral column will not define a man; and we should never use the designation of vertebrate as a synonym of man. That the Spirit is called the "Spirit of faith" means that faith does not exist except as His gift; its very existence is bound up in His working. Just as we call Him the Spirit of life, the Spirit of holiness, and the like, because all life comes from Him and all holiness is of His making, so, when Paul calls Him the Spirit of faith, it is the evidence that in Paul's conception, all faith comes from Him.

It matters not where faith is found— under the Old Testament or the New— in Psalmist or in Apostle— or in the distant believers of the Twentieth Century— it matters not what degree of faith is present, weak, timid faith, which scarcely dares believe in its own existence, or strong faith that can move mountains— it matters not what of divine things be its object, God as our Ruler and Governor, the Scriptures as His Word, Christ as our Savior; if it exists at all, in any time, in any degree, the Holy Spirit has wrought it. He is the Spirit of faith, and faith is His unique product.

Finally, it will be of interest to us who are charged with the same duty of proclaiming the Gospel of salvation with which the Apostle was charged, to take especial note that he attributes that supreme faithfulness and steadfastness which preeminently characterized his work in the Gospel to a Spirit- wrought faith in the Gospel which he preached. The secret, he tells us, of his ability to continue throughout his dreadful trials in the work to which he had been called; the secret of his power to faint not, that is, not to play the coward, but to renounce the hidden things of shame and refuse to walk in craftiness or handle the Word of God deceitfully; the secret of his power to preach a simple Gospel in honest faithfulness in the face of all temptations to please men, and to preach the saving Gospel in the face of all persecution— was simply that he had a hearty and unfeigned faith in it. When we really believe the Gospel of the Grace of God— when we really believe that it is the power of God unto salvation, the only power of salvation in this wicked world of ours— it is a comparatively easy thing to preach it, to preach it in its purity, to preach it in the face of a scoffing, nay, of a truculent and murdering world. Here is the secret— I do not now say of a minister's power as a preacher of God's grace— but of a minister's ability to preach at all this Gospel in such a world as we live in. Believe this Gospel, and you can and will preach it. Let men say what they will, and do what they will— let them injure, ridicule, persecute, slay— believe this Gospel and you will preach it.

Men often say of some element of the Gospel, "I can't preach that." Sometimes they mean that the world will not receive this or that. Sometimes they mean that the world will not endure this or that. Sometimes they mean that they cannot so preach this or that as to win the respect or the sympathy or the acceptance of the world. The Gospel cannot be preached? Cannot be preached? It can be preached if you will believe it. Here is the root of all your difficulties. You do not fully believe this Gospel! Believe it! Believe it! and then it will preach itself! God has not sent us into the world to say the most plausible things we can think of; to teach men what they already believe. He has sent us to preach unpalatable truths to a world lying in wickedness; apparently absurd truths to men, proud of their intellects; mysterious truths to men who are carnal and cannot receive the things of the Spirit of God. Shall we despair? Certainly, if it is left to us not only to plant and to water but also to give the increase. Certainly not, if we appeal to and depend upon the Spirit of faith. Let Him but move on our hearts and we will believe these truths; and, even as it is written, I believed and therefore have I spoken, we also will believe and therefore speak. Let Him but move on the hearts of our hearers and they, too, will believe what He has led us to speak. We cannot proclaim to the world that the house is afire— it is a disagreeable thing to say, scarcely to be risked in the presence of those whose interest it is not to believe it. But believe it, and how quickly you rush forth to shout the unpalatable truth! So believe it and we shall assert to the world that it is lost in its sin and rushing down to an eternal doom; that in Christ alone is there redemption; and through the Spirit alone can men receive this redemption. What care we if it be unpalatable, if it be true? For if it be true, it is urgent.

8

NEW TESTAMENT PURITANISM

2 Corinthians 6:11-7:1— "Our mouth is open unto you, O Corinthians, our heart is enlarged. Ye are not straitened in us, but ye are straitened in your own affections. Now for a recompense in like kind (I speak as unto my children), be ye also enlarged. Be not unequally yoked with unbelievers: for what fellowship have righteousness and iniquity? or what communion hath light with darkness? And what concord hath Christ with Belial? or what portion hath a believer with an unbeliever? And what agreement hath a temple of God with idols? for we are a temple of the living God; even as God said, 'I will dwell in them, and walk in them; and I will be their God, and they shall be My people.' Wherefore, 'come ye out from among them, and be ye separate,' saith the Lord. 'And touch no unclean thing; and I will receive you, and will be to you a Father, and ye shall be to Me sons and daughters,' saith the Lord Almighty. Having therefore these promises, beloved, let us cleanse ourselves from all defilement of flesh and spirit, perfecting holiness in the fear of God."

It is not easy to determine with exactitude the circumstances which gave occasion to this striking paragraph, which stands out so prominently on the pages of 2 Corinthians as almost to separate itself from its context and form a whole of its own. Of two things, however, we may be reasonably sure. There was a party in the Corinthian Church which we may perhaps fairly describe as the party of the Libertines; and out of this party, too, there had arisen an opposition to the leadership of Paul, and a tendency to accuse him of insincerity and self-seeking in his work at Corinth. We must picture the Apostle, therefore, as compelled to defend himself and the purity of his ministry in this Epistle, not only against a narrow Judaistic formalism, with its touch not, taste not, handle not, but also against a loose worldliness which was inclined to adapt its Christianity to the usages current in the heathen society about it. Differing in everything else, both parties agreed in unwillingness to subject themselves unreservedly to the guidance of Paul, and in defense of themselves, represented him as acting toward the church from interested motives.

Bearing this in mind, we may readily understand how, when in the course of his self-defense the Apostle has been led to dwell upon the hardships he had suffered in the prosecution of his mission, he should break off suddenly with an appeal to his Corinthians to separate themselves from heathen practices and points of view, and themselves to walk worthily of the Gospel they professed. "See, O Corinthians," he exclaims, "how freely I am speaking to you, how widely open my heart is to you. You find no constraint on my part with reference to you; the only constraint there is between us lies in your own hearts. Give me what I give you— I am speaking as to my children; open wide your heart to me. Seek not your standards of life in the unbelievers about you. Remember who you are and what you should be as organs of the Holy Spirit; and be not content until you have attained that perfect holiness which becomes the children of God." So the Apostle transforms his defense of his ministry into an exhortation to his readers, in which he again exercises his ministry of love in a disinterested plea to them to walk worthily of the Gospel of holiness.

Dr. James Denney, in his commentary on this Epistle, published in *The Expositor's Bible*, heads the chapter in which he deals with this section, "New Testament Puritanism." On the face of it, this is a very good designation for it. The note of Puritanism, which is the note of separation, certainly throbs through the section. "Come ye out from among them and be ye separate, saith the Lord"— that assuredly expresses the very essence of Puritanism. Or, perhaps, we may more precisely say that it is exactly that conformity with the world which, above all things, Puritanism dreads, that Paul here declares, almost with indignation, to be inconceivable in a true Christian. "For what fellowship," he demands, "is there between righteousness and iniquity? Or what communion is there for light with darkness? Or what concord of Christ with Belial? Or what part has a believer with an unbeliever? Or what agreement has a temple of God with idols?" Here certainly is Puritanism at the height of its expression.

Nevertheless, we must be careful not to give the Apostle's exhortation a turn which does not belong to it. The Apostle is not here requiring of Christians a withdrawal from the world, considered as the social organism; and most certainly he is not asking of them to segregate themselves into a community apart, between which and the mass of men there shall be no, or only the least possible, intercourse. On a former occasion, when addressing these same readers, he does indeed command them not to keep company with fornicators. But he immediately adds that he means this aloofness only as a disciplinary measure toward sinning brethren. If a man who is called a Christian be a fornicator, Christian fellowship must be withdrawn from him that it may be brought home to him that a man cannot be both a Christian and a fornicator. But, says the Apostle, I do not mean that you should not associate with fornicators of the world; else you would need to remove out of the world— a thing, he implies, which would be manifestly impossible; and let us add, for the leaven which is placed in the world, grossly inconsistent with the prosecution of its function in the world, which is to leaven the whole mass. And if we will scrutinize our present passage closely, we shall quickly see that the separation which the Apostle is urging here, too, is not separation from men, but from evil— applying, indeed, to the Corinthians in the way of exhortation what our Lord prayed for in behalf of His followers, not that they should be taken out of the world, but that they should be kept from the evil of the world. The exhortation, "Come ye out from among them and be ye separate, saith the Lord," is immediately followed by the explanation, "And touch no unclean thing." And the whole exhortation closes with a poignant prayer that they may "cleanse themselves from every defilement." It is not from their fellowmen that the Apostle would have Christians hold themselves aloof; it is from the sin and shame, the evil and iniquity, which stains and soils the lives of so many of their fellowmen. This is the Apostolic variety of Puritanism.

The opposite impression is perhaps fostered among simple Bible readers by the phrase which stands in the forefront of the exhortation in our English Bibles: "Be not unequally yoked together with unbelievers." This certainly appears at first sight to represent any commerce with unbelievers as indecorous and to forbid it on that account. This impression is wholly due, however, to the awkwardness of the rendering given to an unusual Greek phrase. This Greek phrase is an exceedingly awkward one to render, and I am not sure that it is possible to give it an English equivalent which will convey its exact sense. The figure which underlies it is, no doubt, the yoking together, in the bizarre way of the East, incongruous animals for labor, say an ox and an ass. And the English version is a very creditable effort to bring the figure home to the English reader, for surely such a yoking of incongruous animals together is a very unequal one. Yet the English phrase fails to express the exact shade of meaning of the Greek term. This does not say, "Be not unequally yoked together with unbelievers," but rather, "Become not bearers of an alien yoke along with unbelievers"— or, in other words, "Take not on yourselves a yoke that does not fit you, in order to be with unbelievers." You see the point is very different from that which is often taken from the English phrase. What is forbidden is not that we should company with unbelievers, but that we should adopt their points of view and their modes of life. It is a question, in other words, not of intercourse, but of standards. What the Apostle is concerned about is not that his converts lived in social communion with their heathen neighbors; this he would have them do. What he is concerned about is that they took their color from the heathen neighbors with whom they lived. He wished them to be leaven and to leaven the lump; they were permitting themselves rather to be leavened; and this made him indignant with them.

We see, then, that the Apostle's urgency here is against, not association with the world, but compromise with the worldly. Compromise! In that one word is expressed a very large part of a Christian's life. We must be all things to all men, we say, perverting the Apostle's prescription for a working ministry; for there was one thing he would on no account and in no way have us be, even that we may, as we foolishly fancy, win the more, and that is, evil. From evil in all its forms and in all its manifestations he would have us absolutely to separate ourselves; the unclean thing is the thing he would in no circumstances have us handle. Associate with the world, yes! There is no man in it so vile that he has not claims upon us for our association and for our aid. But adopt the standards of the world? No! Not in the least particular. Here our motto must be and that unfailingly: No compromise!

The very thing which the Apostle here presses upon our apprehension is the absolute conflict between the standards of the world and the standards of Christians; and the precise thing which he requires of us is that, in our association with the world, we shall not take on our necks the alien yoke of an unbeliever's point of view, of an unbeliever's judgment of things, of an unbeliever's estimate of the right and wrong, the proper and improper. In all our association with unbelievers, we, as Christian men, are to furnish the standard; and we are to stand by our Christian standard, in the smallest particular, unswervingly. Any departure from that standard, however small or however desirable it may seem, is treason to our Christianity. We must not, in any case, take the alien yoke of an unbeliever's scheme of life upon our necks.

Interesting to us as this exhortation itself is, and important beyond expression for the guidance of our lives, it, perhaps, yields in interest to the grounding which the Apostle supplies for it in an explanation of the essential springs of a Christian's life. This grounding he gives in a series of rhetorical questions, by means of which he sets forth the absolute contrariety of the Christian's and the unbeliever's points of view, sources of judgment, and principles of conduct. The ordering of these questions is such that they begin by setting over against one another the obvious contradictions of righteousness and iniquity; and then proceed in a series of rapid and convincing antitheses until they end in setting the believer and the unbeliever over against one another as the embodiment respectively— at least in principle— of those contradictions, righteousness and iniquity. "What fellowship have righteousness and iniquity," the Apostle demands in fellowship have righteousness and iniquity," the Apostle demands in support of his exhortation not to take on themselves the alien yoke of unbelievers, "or," he continues, "what communion has light with darkness? or what concord has Christ with Belial? or what portion has a believer with an unbeliever? or"— clinching the whole matter with a reference to the source of the entire contrast— "what agreement has a temple of God with idols?

"The force of the appeal lies in the necessary— and inevitable— identification, as we go on through the series, of each pair with the preceding; so that with the fundamental "righteousness" is identified the light; and, of course, Christ; and because he is Christ's, the believer, who is the temple of the living God; and with the fundamental iniquity is identified the darkness, Belial, and the unbeliever, because he is the worshipper of idols and partaker of the idolatrous point of view. The reason, then, why a Christian must not take on himself the alien yoke of unbelievers is just because it is to him alien; he is, in and of himself, because a believer in Christ and, therefore, a temple of the living God, a different, a contrary, an opposite kind of being from the unbeliever; and it is, therefore, incongruous in the extreme for him to put his neck in the same yoke with an unbeliever, seek to live on the same plane, or consent to order his life or to determine questions of conduct by his standards in any degree whatever.

Now it is just in this contrast drawn by the Apostle between the believer and the unbeliever— in its firmness, its clearness, its extremity, if you will— that we discern the most interesting, the most important, teaching of our passage. According to the Apostle, obviously there are two kinds of men in the world, believers and unbelievers. And these two kinds of men stand over against one another in complete, not only contrast, but contradiction, as complete contradiction as righteousness and iniquity. There can be no compromise between them any more than between righteousness and iniquity. There may be intercourse— mutual action and reaction— but never compromise.

The Apostle is far from saying, of course, that in any given individuals this fundamental contradiction is fully manifested. It finds its complete manifestation only in the abstract— in the contrariety of righteousness and iniquity, and in the full concrete manifestation of righteousness and iniquity in Christ and Belial. Between Christians and unbelievers the manifested contradiction is only relative. Compromise there ought not to be— in principle there cannot be— but compromise, in fact, there is. Christians are not, like Christ, pure embodiments of righteousness; they require exhortation not to admit iniquity into the governing principles of their life. Alas, alas, though they are temples of the living God, they are far, far from having no commerce with idols. The Apostle recognizes all this. On his recognition of it he founds the urgent exhortation of our passage. Nevertheless he founds this exhortation also on the fact that this contradiction exists in principle— that Christians, like Christ, their Lord, are in principle righteousness, and that unbelievers are, like Belial, their lord, in principle iniquity. It is because Christians are thus in principle holy and unbelievers are thus in principle unholy that he proclaims that it is incongruous that Christians should adopt their standards of life from unbelievers, who are not merely their opposites but their contradictories; so that there can be no mean between them, but everyone must be one or the other.

There are then, according to the Apostle, two kinds of men in the world, believers and unbelievers; and these two kinds of men stand in contradiction to each other. One may conquer and eliminate the other, but there can be no mixture between them. The ultimate source of the fundamental difference between them he finds in the indwelling in Christians of the Holy Spirit: "Or what agreement hath a temple of God with idols? For *we*"— emphatic here, in contrast with the unbelievers, "as for us, *we* are a temple of the living God." The influx of the Holy Spirit into the heart constitutes, then, a new humanity. Over against those who have not the Spirit, and who are, therefore, as another Scripture puts it, earthly, sensual, devilish— the children of Belial, as this Scripture suggests, those who have the Spirit are a new creation, with new standards and new powers of life alike. There can be no compromise between such opposites. It has become customary among theologians to speak of these two kinds of men as the men of nature and the men of the palingenesis; or as it is now becoming fashionable to call them, once born and twice born men. They who are born of the flesh are fleshly; and they only who are born of the Spirit are spiritual; and to the spiritual man belong all things. The message which Paul brings to us in this passage is, then, that we who are spiritual, because we are believers in Christ Jesus, have in principle the righteousness which belongs to Him, and though it may not yet appear what we shall be, we must in all our walk comport ourselves as what we are, the temples of the living God, having the powers and potencies of a new, even a divine, life within us. The ultimate reason why the Christian man is not to compromise with the world is because, as a Christian man, he is a new creature, born from above, with the vigor of the Divine life itself moving in him and with an entirely new life course marked out for him. Why should— how can— such an one put his neck incongruously within the yoke of worldly policy or self-seeking, or evil living with unbelievers, and seek to deflect his Spirit-given powers to a life on this lower plane and for these ignoble ends? O , says the Apostle, O, Christian men, this is surely impossible to you; do you not see that in the power of your new life you are to— you must— take an utterly new course, directed to a new goal and informed with new aspirations, hopes, and strivings?

On the basis of this great declaration the Apostle erects, then, his exhortation. Nor is he content to leave it in a negative or merely inferential form. In the accomplishment of the Spirit-filled life he sees the goal, and he speaks it out in a final urgency of exhortation into which he compresses the whole matter: "Having, therefore, such promises as these (note the emphasis), beloved," he says, "let us purify ourselves from every defilement of flesh and spirit and perfect holiness in the fear of God." It is perfection, we perceive, that the Apostle is after for his followers; and he does not hesitate to raise this standard before the eyes of his readers as their greatest incitement to effort. They must not be content with a moderate attainment in the Christian life. They must not say to themselves, "O, I guess I am Christian enough, although I'm not too good to do as other men do." They must, as they have begun in the Spirit, not finish in the flesh, but must go on unto perfection.

What are they to cleanse themselves from? *Every* defilement— every *kind* of defilement, not only of the flesh but of the spirit. Aiming at what? At the completion of holiness in the fear of God! The Apostle does not tell them they are already holy— except in principle. They obviously were not already holy— except in principle. They were putting their necks in the alien yoke of unbelieving judgments. They were contenting themselves with heathen standards. They were prepared to say, "O, the Lord doesn't ask all that of us; O, there is nothing wrong in this; O, I guess it will be enough if I am as good as the average man; O, you can't expect me to live at odds with all my neighbors; O, these things are good enough for me." Such compromises with the spirit of the world are wrong, and the Apostle tells his readers plainly that they are unworthy of them as Christian men. They were, if not born to better things, yet certainly born anew to better things. Let them turn their backs on all such inconsistencies and live on their own plane of life as believers, believers in Christ, Christ the Light, Christ our Righteousness. Let them remember they are temples of the living God and have no commerce with idols.

No, they were not perfect— except in principle. But in principle, they were perfect; because they had within them the principle of perfection, the Spirit of the Most High God. Let them walk in accordance with their privileges, then, on a level with their destiny. Hear God's great promise. And having these promises, cleanse yourselves; O, cleanse yourselves, the Apostle cries; cleanse yourselves from every defilement, whether of flesh or spirit, and so perfect— complete, work fully out to its end— holiness in the fear of God. Let your standard be the holiness of the indwelling Spirit whose temples you are. Let your motive be, not merely regard to the good of others, much less to your own happiness, but joy in God's gracious promises. Let your effort be perfect sanctification of soul and body, cleansing; from all defilement. Let your end be, pleasing God, the Holy One. In a word, says the Apostle, in effect, here as elsewhere: O, ye Christians, work out your own salvation in fear and trembling, for it is God who is working in you the willing and the doing according to His own good pleasure.

We perceive, thus, in the end that the thing Paul is zealous for is the holiness of his followers. For in their holiness he sees the substance of their salvation. We are saved by Christ and only Christ; and Christ is righteous, both for us and unto us. For it is by grace that we are saved, through faith; and that not of ourselves, it is the gift of God— not out of works, lest we should boast, but unto good works, which God has before prepared that we should walk in them. And if we walk not in them— are we, then, saved? Holiness of life is, I repeat, precisely the substance of salvation, that which we are saved to, that in which salvation consists. If then we are in Christ Jesus, shall we not live like Christ Jesus? "If we are in the Spirit, shall we not walk by the Spirit?" This is Paul's final exhortation to us; since we are Christ's, and the Spirit dwells in us and we are the temples of the living God, let us be careful of good works; let us, remembering the great promises He has given us, cleanse ourselves from all defilement of body and soul; and let us perfect holiness in the fear of God, so that we approve ourselves His children, and He will be to us as a Father, and we shall be to Him sons and daughters.

9

SPIRITUAL STRENGTHENING

Ephesians 3:14-19, especially 16— "That He would grant you, according to the riches of His glory, that ye may be strengthened with power through His Spirit in the inward man."

This certainly may be fairly called one of the great passages of the Bible. Note the series of great topics which are adverted to in it: the inward strengthening of the children of God by the Holy Spirit, the continual abiding of Christ in their hearts, their rooting and grounding in love, their enlargement in spiritual apprehension, even to the knowledge of the unknowable, their filling with all the fullness of God. Surely here is a catalogue of great things for God's people! These great topics do not lie on one level, however, set side by side as parallel facts, but are exhibited in special relations, the one to the other. Paul is praying here for these high blessings to descend on the Ephesian Christians. But he does not pray for them simply as a bunch of blessings, arbitrarily selected to be on this occasion sought at the great Father's hands— the Father of these Ephesian Christians too, because He is the God of the Gentiles as well as of the Jews, and from Him every fatherhood derives its name. Here are rather a connected body of blessings which go naturally together, one being the ground and another the effect of the one great thing he craves for his readers.

The central thing he prays for is spiritual strengthening. "I bow my knees to the Father that He may give to you to be strengthened by His Spirit in respect to the inner man." Spiritual strengthening, then, that is the main thing that he prays for. By the mere term "spiritual strengthening," two things might be suggested to us. We might think of spiritual as distinguished from physical strengthening. Or we might think of strengthening by the Spirit as distinguished from some earthly agency. The Apostle's prayer includes both ideas. He prays that we may be strengthened in the inner man, that is, for the strengthening of our spirit, in distinction from the body. And he prays that we may be strengthened with respect to the inner man by God's Spirit, that is, for the divine strengthening of our inward man. And this, I say, is the substance of his prayer— that we may be strengthened with respect to the inner man by the Spirit of God. All else is descriptive of this and tells us what it is, and what it results in, and so enhances our idea of what spiritual strengthening is.

First, Paul tells us somewhat further what it is. It is identical, he tells us, with the abiding of Christ by faith in our hearts. Of course it is not absolutely certain what the relation of this second clause is to its predecessor. It might express the aim or end of the spiritual strengthening, or (what comes to practically the same thing) its result, as well as (as we should take it) its more precise explanation. As it is followed by a series of expressly telic[6] clauses, formally introduced by the proper telic particle, it would seem most natural to take it as epexegetical[7] of the preceding clause. "I bow my knees to the Father . . . that He may give to you, according to the riches of His glory, to be strengthened with might as to the inner man— to wit, that Christ may abide in your hearts by faith." To be sure, the sense would not be essentially different if we took it otherwise— to the end that, or so that, Christ may abide in your hearts by faith. In the one case, it tells what the spiritual strengthening consists in— it is identical with the abiding of Christ in the heart; in the other, what it eventuates in— it issues in the abiding of Christ in the heart. In either case, the thing to be noted is that it is not the coming of Christ into the heart that is spoken of, but His abiding in the heart; and that it is just this idea that receives the emphasis in the sentence, the position of the words being such as to throw a strong stress on " abiding."

Spiritual Strengthening

Two things result from this. The first is that Christ is supposed to have already entered the hearts of those whom the Apostle is praying for. It is not a question of His coming but of His abiding. The Apostle is not praying that his readers should be converted; but, presuming their conversion, that they may be spiritually strengthened. The second result is that the spiritual strengthening is contingent on, or let us rather say, is dependent on the abiding presence of Christ in their hearts. The indwelling Christ is the source of the Christian's spiritual strength. This is, of course, not to set aside the Holy Spirit. But he has read his New Testament to little purpose who would separate the Holy Spirit and Christ: Christ abides in the heart by the Spirit. The indwelling of the Holy Spirit is the means of the indwelling of Christ, and the two are one and the same great fact. We are strengthened in the inner man with might by the Holy Spirit because, by the operation of the Spirit in our hearts, Christ abides there— thus and not otherwise. And here we learn then the source of the Christian's strength. Christ is the ultimate source. His indwelling is the ground of all our strength. But it is only by the Spirit— the executive of the Godhead in this sphere too— that Christ dwells in the heart. It is the Spirit that strengthens us, and He so strengthens us that He gives us "might" in our inner man. The way He does this is by forming Christ within us.

The Apostle is one of the most fecund writers extant, and thus it happens that he does not leave the matter even there. It is by the Spirit that Christ dwells in us— that is the objective fact. But there is a subjective fact too, and the Apostle does not fail to touch it— it is by our faith, too, that Christ dwells in us. "That Christ may abide in your hearts by your faith," he says. He does not say "by faith" merely, though he might well have said that, and it would have covered the whole necessary idea. But in his habitual fullness of expression, he puts in the article and thus implies that he recognizes their faith as already existent. They are Christians, they already believe, Christ is already dwelling in them by faith; he prays that He may abide in them by their faith. The stress is everywhere laid on continuance. May God strengthen your inner man, he says, by His Spirit. That is to say, he adds, may that Christ whom ye have received into your hearts by faith abide continuously in your hearts by that faith of yours. As much as to say, Christ is brought into your hearts by the Holy Spirit. He abides there by that Holy Spirit. May God thus continually strengthen your hearts by His Spirit, and that, even with might. I pray to Him for it, for it is He that gives it. But do not think, therefore, that you may lose hold on Christ. It is equally true that He abides in your hearts by your faith. When faith fails, so do the signs of His presence within; the strengthening of the Spirit and the steady burning of the flame of faith are correlative. As well expect the thermometer to stand still with the temperature varying as the height of your faith not to index the degree of your strength. Your strength is grounded in the indwelling Christ, wrought by the Spirit by means of faith.

Thus we have laid before us the sources of the Christian strength. It is rooted in Christ, the Christ within us abiding there by virtue of the Spirit's action quickening and upholding faith in us. And only, as by the Spirit our faith is kept firm and clear, will Christ abide in us and will we accordingly be strong in the inner man.

Such then is the nature and source of the Christian's strengthening. What does it issue in? How does it exhibit itself? Briefly, the Apostle tells us, in love and knowledge. "May God grant you," he says "to be strengthened as to the inner man by His Spirit, that is, the abiding presence of Christ in your heart, to the end that being rooted and grounded in love, you may be fully enabled to apprehend..." The end of the prayer is, then, expansion of spiritual apprehension. May God grant that you may be strengthened with might... to the end that you may be full of strength to apprehend. The appropriate result of strengthening is that they may have full strength. The Apostle accumulates words expressive of strength to enhance the idea. He uses three separate words but all impinging on the one idea, that he wishes his readers, by the Holy Spirit's operations, to be raised to the capacity of spiritual apprehension indicated. "God grant that ye may be empowered (relative and manifested power) with might (inherent general power), with which ye may have full strength (as your own endowment) to apprehend..." This then is the proximate end of the prayer: Expansion of heart for the apprehension of spiritual things. "God grant that you may be strengthened with might by the Holy Spirit in the inner man, that you may have full strength to apprehend..." These things to be apprehended are too great for man's natural powers. He must have new strength from on high given him to compass them. He may by the Spirit be raised to a higher potency of apprehension for them. God grant it to you!

What are these things? The Apostle speaks quite generally about them. He says, "that ye may have full strength to apprehend with all the saints what is the breadth and length and height and depth. . ." His mind is, for the moment, not on the thing itself but on the bigness of the thing. It is because the thing is so big that they need strengthening in the inner man before they have full strength to apprehend it. Yet it is not something for these special readers alone, but for all Christians. This strengthening the Apostle asks for is the heritage of the saints. The Apostle prays not that we may be expanded in spiritual apprehension by these great ideas, but up to them. This expanding is not to be done by them, but by the Holy Spirit. To enhance our conception of how big they are, he gives us a sample— for that the last clause here is not adjoined as a parallel but as a subordinate clause seems indicated by the particle by which it is adjoined and as well by the concluding words "unto the whole fullness of God," which appear to return to a quite general idea: that ye may have full strength to apprehend with all saints what is the breadth and length and height and depth and to know the "knowledge-surpassing love of Christ."

Here is a sample of the broad and wide and high and deep knowledge to apprehend which we need to have our minds stretched, the quality of the love of Christ. It is too high for us; we cannot attain unto it. Do we wonder that the thing the Apostle prays for is that we should be strengthened in the inner man by the Spirit of God, that we may have full strength to apprehend this? Do we wonder that he speaks of this and such knowledge as too broad and wide and high and deep for us, not to be apprehended save by him in whose heart Christ abides? If, indeed, Christ be in us— then, possibly, we may know Christ without us. But surely in no other way. Here then is the gist of the matter, as to the end of our strengthening in the inner man. It is to give us full strength for the apprehension of these great and incomparable mysteries of our faith.

But in that fullness of the Apostle's speech to which we have already alluded, Paul does not content himself with simply saying this. He so says it as both to suggest an intermediate step in the attainment of this large spiritual apprehension, and to indicate a still higher goal. He suggests, I say, an intermediate step. He does not say simply, "God grant you spiritual strengthening, that you may have enlarged spiritual apprehension." He says, "God grant you spiritual strengthening that, having been rooted and grounded in love, you may have enlarged spiritual apprehension." Here then is an intermediate link between the strengthening by the Spirit and the enlargement of our spiritual understanding. It is "love." The proximate effect of the Spirit's work in empowering the inner man with might is not knowledge, but love; and the proximate cause of our enlarged spiritual apprehension is not the strengthening of our inner man, but love. The Spirit does not immediately work this enlargement of mind in us; He immediately works love, and only through working this love, enlarges our apprehension. The Holy Spirit "sheds love abroad in our hearts." Love is the great enlarger. It is love which stretches the intellect. He who is not filled with love is necessarily small, withered, shriveled in his outlook on life and things. And conversely, he who is filled with love is large and copious in his apprehensions. Only he can apprehend with all saints what is the breadth and length and height and depth of things. The order of things in spiritual strengthening is therefore: (1) the working by the Spirit of a true faith in the heart, and the cherishing by the Spirit of this faith in a constant flame; (2) the abiding of Christ by this faith in the heart; (3) the shedding abroad of love in the soul and its firm rooting in the heart; (4) the enlargement of the spiritual apprehension to know the unknowable greatness of the things of Christ.

There is yet one further step, for even this spiritual apprehension is not its own end. "God grant," says the Apostle, "that you may be empowered with might by the Spirit, so to have full strength to apprehend the great things of God"— but he does not stop there. He adds, "to the end that you may be filled unto the whole fullness of God." Here is the goal at last. And what a goal it is! We were weak— for it was "when we were without strength" that Christ died for us. We are to be strengthened, strengthened by the Spirit, by means of the constant indwelling of Christ, the source of all good. We are to be strengthened so as to know, to know the great things of God (read some of them in the parallel passage, Col. 1:11). But not that we may know for the mere sake of knowing. What good would such a bare knowing do us? We are to know that we may be "filled unto all the fullness of God. Look at this standard of fullness. "Unto"— not "with"— it is the standard, not the material. God's fullness is not to be poured into us; we are to be raised toward that standard of fullness, not in one particular, but in all— unto the whole fullness of God. It may mean unto the fullness which God possesses, or it may mean unto the fullness which He provides. It may mean either that the enlargement of our spiritual apprehension is a means toward obtaining all the wonderful goods that God has in store for us; or it may mean that by it we shall be brought to a height of attainment comparable only to His attainments. No matter which it means. It is enough in either meaning for any Christian's hope. But there is no reason to doubt that it does mean the greatest thing: we shall be filled unto the whole fullness of God. We shall be like Him, and like Him only of all beings in the universe. It is a giddy height to which our eyes are thus raised. No wonder we need spiritual strengthening to discern the summit of this peak of promise.

Of course it does not mean that we are to be transmuted into God, so that each of us will be able to assert a right to a place of equality in the universe with God. Of course, again, it does not mean that God is to be transfused into us, so that we shall be God, part of His very essence. It means just what it says, that God presents the standards toward which we, Christian men, are to be assimilated. We are to be made like Him, holy as He is holy, pure as He is pure. Our eyes, even in the depths of eternity, will seek Him towering eternally above us as our unattainable standard toward which we shall ever be ascending, but we shall be like Him; He and we shall belong to one class, the class of holy beings. We shall no longer be like the devil, whose children we were until we were delivered from his kingdom and translated into the kingdom of God's dear Son. No more shall we be what we were as men in this world, still separated from God by a gulf of moral difference, a difference so great that we are almost tempted to call it a difference of kind and not merely of degree. Nay, we shall, perhaps, be more like God than even the holy angels are; in our head, Christ Jesus, we shall be in Him who, in a preeminent sense, is like God. The process of the "filling" may take long; it is but barely begun for most of us in this life, but that is the standard and that the goal— "we shall be filled unto the fullness of God;" and it shall never cease. Such is the goal of the spiritual strengthening spoken of in our text.

10

THE SEALING OF THE HOLY SPIRIT

Ephesians 4:30 — "And grieve not the Holy Spirit of God, in whom ye were sealed unto the day of redemption."

It is Paul's custom in his epistles to prepare for exhortation by the enunciation of truth; to lay first the foundation of fact and doctrine, and on that foundation to raise his appeals for conduct. The Epistle to the Ephesians is no exception to this rule. The former chapters of this epistle are a magnificent exposition of doctrine, a noble presentation to Paul's readers of what God has done for them in election and redemption and calling, and of the great privileges which they have obtained in Christ. To this he adjoins, according to his custom, a ringing appeal, based on this exposition of truth and privilege. This appeal to his readers is to live up to their privileges, or, in his own words, to walk worthily of the calling wherewith they were called. The whole latter or practical part of the letter is thus expressly based on the former or doctrinal part. And this is true of the exhortations in detail as well as in general. Paul wrote always with vital connectedness. There never was a less artificial writer, and none of his epistles bears more evident traces than the Epistle to the Ephesians of having been written, as the Germans say, "at a single gush." All here is of a piece, and part is concatenated with part in the intimate connection which arises out of— not artificial effort to obtain logical consecution— but the living flow of a heart full of a single purpose.

Take, as an example, the beautiful appeal of our text. The Apostle is not perfunctorily or mechanically repeating a set phrase, a pious platitude. He is making an appeal, out of a full heart, to just the readers he has in mind, in just their situation; and under the impulse of his own vivid appreciation of their peculiar state and condition. On the basis of the privileges they had received in Christ, he had exhorted them generally to an accordant inner and outer conduct; and he had presented these general exhortations both positively and negatively. Now he has come to details. He has enumerated several of the sins to which they in their situation were liable, perhaps, in a special degree, sins of falsehood, wrath, theft, unbecoming speech. Shall they, even they, the recipients of this new life and all these divine favors, fall into such sins? He suddenly broadens the appeal into an earnest beseeching not so to grieve the Holy Spirit of God in whom they were sealed unto the day of redemption. That they, too, had this sealing, had he not just told them? Nay, had he not just pointed them to it as to their most distinguishing grace? It is not by a new or a merely general motive by which he would move their hearts. It is distinctly by the motive to which he had already adverted and which he had made their own. It was because he had taught them to understand and feel that they, even they, Gentiles according to the flesh, had been sealed with the Holy Spirit of promise as an earnest of their inheritance, and could count on this being a living and moving motive in their minds— or rather it is because he himself felt this great truth as real and as a motive of power— that he adduces it here to move them to action.

If we are to feel the motive power in the appeal as Paul felt it and as he desired his readers to feel it, we must approach it as he approached it and as he desired them to approach it, namely, through a preliminary apprehension and appreciation of the fact underlying the appeal and giving it force. To do this we should approach the consideration of the text under some such logical analysis of its contents as the following. First, we should consider the great fact on which the appeal is based, namely, that Christians have been sealed by the Holy Spirit unto the day of redemption. Secondly, we should consider the nature of this sealing Spirit as the Holy Spirit, and the pain which all sin must bring to Him as the indwelling and sealing Spirit. Thirdly, we should consider the nature and strength of the motive thence arising to us, who are the recipients of His grace, to refrain from the sin which grieves Him, and to seek the life of holiness which pleases Him. Time would fail us, however, on this occasion fully to develop the contents of these propositions. Let us confine ourselves to a few brief remarks on (1) the nature of the basal fact on which Paul founds his appeal as to our position as Christians; and (2) the nature of the motive which he seeks to set in action by his appeal.

The fundamental fact on which Paul, in the text, bases his appeal to a holy life is that his readers, because Christians, "have been sealed in the Holy Spirit unto the day of redemption." Now, "sealing" expresses authentication or security, or perhaps we may say, authentication and security. It is then, the security of the Christian's salvation which is the fact appealed to; the Christian is "sealed," authenticated as a redeemed one, and made secure as to the completion of the redemption, for he is sealed unto the day of redemption.

The reference to Paul's teaching in a former chapter, as to the grace given to his readers, will help us to understand the fact here adduced as a motive to action. There we have the fuller statement that these Christians had heard the Word of the Truth, the Gospel of salvation, preached to them; that they had heard it and had believed it; and then, that they had been "sealed with the Holy Spirit of promise," in other words the Holy Spirit who works out all the promises to us to fruition; "who," adds the Apostle, "is an earnest of our inheritance," an earnest being more than a pledge, inasmuch as it is both a pledge and a part of the inheritance itself. Then the Apostle tells us unto what we were thus sealed by the Holy Spirit of promise, who is Himself an earnest of our inheritance, namely, "unto the redemption of God's own possession unto the praise of His glory."

Let us read these great words backwards that we may grasp their full import. Christians are primarily the purchased possession of God: God has purchased them to Himself by the precious blood of His Son. But the purchase is one thing and "the delivery of the goods" another. Their redemption is, therefore, not completed by the simple purchase. There remains, accordingly, a "day of redemption" yet in the future, unto which the purchased possession is to be brought. Meanwhile, because we are purchased and are God's possession, we are sealed to Him and to the fulfillment of the redemption to take place on that day. And the seal is the Holy Spirit here designated as the "Holy Spirit of promise" because it is through Him that the promise is to be fulfilled; and the "earnest of our inheritance," because He is both the pledge that the inheritance shall be ours and a foretaste of that inheritance itself. The whole is a most pointed assertion that those who have been bought by the blood of Christ, and brought to God by the preached Gospel, shall be kept by His power unto the salvation which is ready to be revealed at the last day.

The great fact on which Paul bases his appeal is, therefore, the fact of the security of believers, of the preservation by God of His children, of the "perseverance of the saints"— to use time-honored theological language. We are sealed, rendered secure, by the Holy Spirit unto the day of redemption: we are sealed by the Holy Spirit, the fulfiller of the promises, and the earnest of our inheritance, unto the full redemption of us, who are God's purchased possession. The fact the Apostle adverts to is, in a word, that our salvation is sure.

How is this a motive to holiness? Men say that security acts rather as a motive to carelessness. Well, we observe at least that the Apostle does not think so, but uses it rather as a motive to holiness. Because we have been sealed by the Spirit of God, he reasons, let us not grieve Him by sin. Men may think that a stronger appeal might be based on fear lest we fall from the Spirit's keeping; as if Paul should rather have said, "Because you can be kept only by the Spirit, beware lest you grieve Him away by sinning." But Paul's actual appeal is not to fear but to gratitude. Because you have been sealed by the Spirit unto the day of redemption, see to it that you do not grieve, bring pain or sorrow to this Spirit, who has done so much for you.

It is not to be denied, of course, that the motive of fear is a powerful one, a legitimate one to appeal to, and one which, in its due place, is appealed to constantly in the Scriptures. It is, no doubt, a relatively lower motive than that here appealed to by Paul; but as Bishop Doane once truly said, "most men are more amenable to appeals addressed to the lower than to those addressed to the higher motives." When men cease to be of a low mind, we can afford to deal with them on a higher plane. I have no sympathy, therefore, with the view, often expressed, that man must not be urged to save his soul by an appeal to his interests, by an appeal to the joys of heaven or to the pains of torment. You all know the old story of how St. Iddo once, when he journeyed abroad, met an old crone with a pitcher of water in one hand and a torch ablaze in the other, who explained that the torch was to burn up heaven and the water to quench hell, that men might no longer seek to please God because of desire for one or fear of the other, but might be led only by disinterested love. History says that St. Iddo went home wondering. Well he might. For on such teachings as this he should have to forego the imitation of his Lord, who painted to men the delights of the heavenly habitations and forewarned men to fear him who has power after he has destroyed the body also to cast into hell, where, so He says, "their worm dieth not and the fire is not quenched." The motives of fear of punishment and vision of reward, though relatively low motives, are yet legitimate motives, and are, in their own place, valuable.

But the Apostle teaches us in our present passage that the higher motives, too, are for use and, in their own place, are the motives to use. Do not let us, as Christian ministers, assume that our flocks, purchased by the blood of Christ, and sealed unto the day of redemption by the Spirit, are accessible only to the lowest motives. "Give a dog a bad name," says the proverb, "and hang him." And the proverb may be an allegory to us. Deal with people on a low plane, and they may sink to that plane and become incapable of occupying any other. Cry to them, "Lift up your hearts," and believe me, you will obtain your response. It is a familiar experience that if you treat a man as a gentleman, he will tend to act like a gentleman; if you treat him like a thief, only the grace of God and strong moral fiber can hold him back from stealing. Treat Christian men like Christian men; expect them to live on Christian principles; and they will strive to walk worthily of their Christian profession.

So far from Paul's appeal to the high motive of gratitude here, then, being surprising, it is, even on the low ground of natural psychology, true and right. The highest motives are relatively the most powerful. And when we leave the low ground of natural psychology and take our stand on the higher ground of Christian truth, how significant and instructive it is. If the Holy Spirit has done this for me; if He in all His holiness is dwelling in me to seal me unto the day of redemption, shall I have no care not to grieve Him? Fear is paralyzing. Despair is destruction of effort. Hope is living and active in every limb, and when that hope becomes assurance, and that assurance is recognized as based on the act of a Person lovingly dealing with us and winning us to holiness, can we conceive of a motive to holiness of equal power?

Brethren, we must not speak of such things historically only. We are not here simply to observe how Paul appealed to the Ephesians, as he sought to move them to holy endeavor; nor to discuss whether or not this is a moving manner of dealing with human souls. His appeal is to *us*. The fact asserted is true of *us*— *we* are sealed by the Holy Spirit to the day of redemption. He is in *us*, too, as the Holy Spirit whom sin offends, and as the loving Spirit who is working in *us* toward good. Do *we* feel the pull of the appeal? Shall *we* listen to and feel and yield to and obey Paul's great voice crying to *us* down through the ages: "Grieve not the Holy Spirit of God in whom ye were sealed unto the day of redemption"? Commune with your souls on these things today!

11

THE WAY OF LIFE

Titus 3:4-7— **"But when the kindness of God, our Savior, and His love towards man, appeared, not by works done in righteousness, which we did ourselves, but according to His mercy He saved us, through the washing of regeneration and renewing of the Holy Spirit, which He poured out upon us richly, through Jesus Christ our Savior; that being justified by His grace, we might be made heirs according to the hope of eternal life."**

The short epistle to Titus contains, amid its practical and ecclesiastical directions for the giving of which it was written, two doctrinal statements of quite wonderful richness and compression, both of which have been easily brought into the compass of the passage read in your hearing this afternoon (see Tit. 2:11-3:8). They differ from each other in intent and content, as you will doubtless have observed. But they are alike in gathering into the narrow space of a few words the essence of the Gospel, and expressing it in words of a singularly festal and jubilant character, words which strike the reader as at once precise and comprehensive, as at once theologically exact and peculiarly fitted for public creedal use.

Statements of this kind are characteristic of these latest epistles of the Apostle Paul, which we class together under the common title of the Pastoral Epistles, and which share not only the late origin at the end of Paul's life when he was busied with consolidating and extending the churches he had founded rather than with the first planting of Christianity in the fresh soil of an unbelieving world. They present the doctrines of Paul, after they had been used, and worn round by use. They represent the sifting down of his doctrinal expositions into compact form; their compression into something like pebbles from the brook ready to be flung with sure aim and to sink into the foreheads of the Goliaths of unbelief. They represent the form which his doctrinal expositions had taken as current coin in the churches, no longer merely Paul's teaching, though all of that, but the precious possessions of the people themselves, in which they were able to give back to him a response of their listening hearts. They are no longer mere dialectical elaboration of the truth, but have become forms of sound words. As such, such passages are accompanied by a phrase peculiar to these Pastoral Epistles, which advertises these statements as something other than a teacher's novel presentations of truth to as yet untaught hearers: "This is a faithful saying." "This is a faithful saying"— a "trustworthy saying"— in other words, this is a saying well-known among you, that has been long repeated in your ears, that has been tested and found not wanting. This is good coin; and "worthy," it is sometimes added, "of all acceptation."

Our present passage is one of these "faithful sayings." "Faithful is the saying," the Apostle adds on completing it, "and concerning these things, I will that thou shouldst affirm confidently." Thus he tells us how important, how well considered, how final and trustworthy this statement of truth is. Let us approach its study in a spirit suitable to so solemn an injunction.

The first thing that we observe in the passage is the melody that rises from it of praise to God. It is the "kindness of God our Savior and His love toward men" which sets its key note. The special terms in which God's goodness is here praised, His "benignity" and "philanthropy," are due, indeed, to the context. The Apostle had just been thinking and speaking about men, and he could not think or speak of them as either "benignant" or "philanthropic." He would have them exhorted to be subject to those over them, obedient, prone to good works, and averse to evil speaking and contentiousness, gentle and meek. But such they were not showing themselves. Christians themselves could remember how beforehand they lived in malice and envy, hateful and hating one another. What could be expected from man? What a contrast when one lifted his eyes from this scene of lust and malice and envy and hatred— men striving with one another to surpass each other in doing injury to their fellows— and set them on God, to see His benignity and philanthropy! The whole passage is pervaded by the suggestion of God's kindness and humanity, thrown out into sharp relief by its contrast with man's malice and hatred. Nothing can be expected of or from man, but God has manifested His benignity and philanthropy to us and by them saved us. Man would destroy; God saves.

But there is much more than this to be said. The passage is not only pervaded by the suggestion of God's general goodness; it is a psalm of praise to God for His saving love. It sings not only "Gloria Deo," but "Soli Deo Gloria." Our salvation is its subject. It not only ascribes salvation in its roots to God's love; it ascribes it in every one of its details to God's loving activities and to them alone; it ascribes its beginning and middle and end to Him and to Him only. The various activities that enter into our salvation are enumerated, and every one of them is declared to be a loving activity of God and of Him alone. This passage is even remarkable in this respect. Even in that classical passage in Ephesians (2:1-10), which is designed to ascribe salvation wholly to God, and to empty man of all ground of boasting, we have faith, at least, mentioned: "We are saved by grace, through faith"; though it is immediately added: "And that not of ourselves, it is the gift of God." But this passage leaves faith itself to one side as not requiring mention. There are no subjective conditions to salvation, in the sense of conditions which we must perform in order to obtain or retain salvation. It is God alone who saves, "not by means of any works in righteousness which we have done ourselves but in consequence of His mercy" and of that alone. Not even faith itself, that instrument of reception to which salvation comes, can be conceived of as entering casually into God's saving work. It is He and He alone who saves; and the roots of His saving operations are set deep in His mercy only. If we are saved at all, it is because— not that we have worked, not that we have believed— but that God has manifested His benignity and philanthropy in saving us out of His mere mercy. He has, through Jesus Christ, shed down His Holy Spirit to regenerate and renovate us that we might be justified "by His grace"— in other words, gratuitously, not on the ground of our faith— and so be made heirs of eternal life.

Our passage empties man of all glory in the matter of salvation and reserves all the glory to God. But this is not because it does not know how to distribute honor to whom honor is due. Man has no part in the procuring or in the applying of salvation, but there are three Persons who have; and our passage recognizes the praise due to each and distributes to each Person of the Holy Trinity the saving operations which belong to Him. "*God...* according to His mercy, ... saved us, through the washing of regeneration and renewal of the *Holy Spirit*, which He poured out on us richly through *Jesus Christ* our Savior." The source of our salvation is to be sought in the loving mercy of God the Father. The ground of the saving activities exerted on us is to be sought in the Holy Spirit. Here are brought before us God our Lover, Christ our Redeemer, the Spirit our Sanctifier, as all operative in the one composite work of salvation. To God the Father is ascribed the whole scheme of salvation and the entire direction of the saving work; it is His benignity and philanthropy that are manifested in it; it is according to His own mercy that He has saved us; it is He that saved us; He saved us through the Holy Spirit; He poured out the Holy Spirit through Jesus Christ; it is His salvation, and it is He that has given it to us. To Jesus Christ is ascribed the work of "Savior," by which the outpouring of the Holy Spirit was rendered possible to God. The nature of His work is not precisely outlined in our passage; but in the preceding passage we are told that "He gave Himself for us, that He might redeem us from all iniquity." This it is that the Son does for us. To the Holy Spirit is ascribed the actual application of the redemption wrought out by Christ. The items of this application are very richly developed, and the development of them constitutes the strength of the passage.

If we will scrutinize the items in which the applying work of the Holy Spirit is developed, we shall perceive that they supply us with a complete "order of salvation." We are told that God saves us in His mere mercy, by a renovating work of the Holy Spirit, founded on the redeeming work of Christ; and we are told that this renovating work of the Holy Spirit was in order that we might be justified and so become heirs. Here the purchase by the death of Christ is made the condition precedent of the regeneration of the Holy Spirit; but the action of the Holy Spirit is made the condition precedent to justification and adoption. We are bought unto God by Christ in order that we may be brought to God by the Holy Spirit. And in bringing us to God, the Holy Spirit precedes by regenerating us in order that we be justified so as to be made heirs. In theological language, that is expressed by saying that the impetration of salvation precedes its application; the Spirit works by first regenerating the soul, next justifying it, next adopting it into the family of God, and next sanctifying it. In the more vital and less analytical language of our present passage, this is asserted by founding the gift of the Holy Spirit upon the work of Christ, "which He poured out upon us richly through Jesus Christ our Savior," by including in the work of the Holy Spirit, regeneration, justification, adoption, and a few verses lower down, sanctification, and by declaring that the regeneration of the Holy Spirit is "in order that being justified we might be heirs."

Now what are the practical fruits of this teaching? The Apostle says it is faithful teaching, which he wishes to have confidently affirmed, to the end that they which have believed God may be careful to maintain good works. It is encouraging teaching to believers to tell them that they are not their own saviors, but God is their Savior; that their salvation is not suspended on their own works or the strength of their own faith, but on the strength of God's love and His mercy alone; that all three Persons of the Trinity are engaged in and pledged to their salvation; that Christ's work for them is finished, and they are redeemed to God by His precious blood and are, henceforth, God's purchased possession; that it is not dependent on their own weakness, but on the Spirit's strength, whether they will be brought into the enjoyment of their salvation; that the Spirit has been poured richly out among them; that He has begun His work of renovation within them; that this is but the pledge of the end and, as they have been regenerated and justified, so have they been brought into the family of God and made heirs of eternal life. This is encouraging teaching for believers! Shall they, then, because they are saved out of God's mercy and not out of works in righteousness which they have done themselves, be careless to maintain good works? I think not; and the Apostle thinks not. Because of this, they will now be careful "to maintain good works." Let us see to it, then, that by so doing we approve ourselves as true believers, saved by God's grace, not out of works but unto good works, which He has before prepared that we should walk in them! This is what the Apostle would have us do.

12

THE LOVE OF
THE HOLY SPIRIT

James 4:5— " Do ye think that the Scripture saith in vain, Thy spirit that dwelleth in us lusteth to envy?"

The translators have found some difficulty in rendering this verse. The form in which I have just read it, is that given it by our Authorized Version. I am not sure that it will at once convey the meaning. The Revised Version, in text and margin, presents several renderings. Among them, there is one which expresses much more clearly what seems to me to be the meaning of the original. It is this: "Or think ye that the Scripture saith in vain, That Spirit which He made to dwell in us yearneth for us even unto jealous envy?" Read thus, in accordance with the context, it is not too much to say that we have here one of the most precious texts in the Bible. It is a declaration, on the basis of Old Testament teaching, of the deep yearning which the Holy Spirit, which God has caused to dwell in us, feels for our undivided and unwavering devotion.

In the context James has been speaking of the origin of the unseemly quarrels which even in that early day, it seems, marred the life of Christians. He traces them to greediness for the pleasures of this world and consequent envy toward those who are better placed or more fortunate in the pursuit of worldly goods. Then he turns suddenly to administer a sorrowful rebuke to the gross inconsistency of such envious rivalry in grasping after the pleasures of this world, for men who possess the inestimable treasure of God's love. It is at

97

once observable on reading over the passage that its whole phraseology is colored by the underlying presentation of the relation of
the Christian to God under the figure of marriage.

The Christian is the bride of God. And, therefore, any commerce
with the world is unfaithfulness. There is not room in this relation
for two loves. To love the world in any degree is a breach of our
vows to our one Husband, God. Hence the exclamation of "Adul-
teresses!" which springs to James' lips when he thinks of Christians
loving the world. Hence his indignant outcry, " Know ye not that
love of the world is enmity with God?" and his sweeping explanation, "Whosoever, therefore, has it in his mind to be a lover of the
world is thereby constituted an enemy of God." We cannot have
two husbands; and to the one husband to whom our vows are
plighted, all our love is due. To dally with the thought of another
lover is already unfaithfulness. On the other side, God is the Husband of the Christian's soul. And He loves it with that peculiar,
constant, changeless love with which one loves what the Scripture
calls his own body (Eph. 5:25-28). Is the soul faithful to Him? Who
can paint, then, the delight He takes in it? Is it unfaithful, turning
to seek its pleasure in the love of the world? Then the Scripture
tells us that it is with jealous yearning that God, its lawful Husband,
looks upon it. Does it, after unfaithfulness, turn again to its rightful
lord? It cannot draw nearer to Him than He is ready to draw to it;
and it no sooner humbles itself before Him than He exalts it.

The general meaning of the text is thus revealed to us as a strong
asseveration of the love of God for His people, set forth under the
figure of a faithful husband's yearning love for his erring bride.
James presents this asseveration of God's love for His people, we
will observe, as the teaching of Scripture; that is, since he was in the
act of penning the earliest of New Testament books, as the teaching
of the Old Testament Scriptures. The mode in which he makes this
appeal to Scripture is perhaps worthy of incidental remark. "Or
think ye that it is an empty saying of Scripture?" The question is a
rhetorical one, and amounts to the strongest assertion that, from
James' point of view, no saying of Scripture could be empty. He
would confound his readers by adducing the tremendous authority
of Scripture in support of his declaration; and therein he reveals to

us the attitude of humble submission toward the Scripture word which characterizes all the writers of the New Testament.

It was not, however, the doctrine of inspiration which was then engaging his thought. He sends us to these inspired Scriptures rather for the doctrine of God's unchanging love toward His sinful people. And we will surely have no difficulty in recalling numerous Old Testament passages in which the Lord has been pleased graciously to express His love for His people under the figure of the love of a husband for his chosen bride; or in which He has been pleased to make vivid to us His sense of the injury done to His love by the unfaithfulness of His people, by attributing to Himself the burning jealousy of a loving husband toward the tenderly cherished wife who has wandered from the path of fidelity. Already this representation underlies expressions which occur in the Pentateuch, and indeed it is enshrined for us in the fabric of the Ten Commandments themselves, where God announces Himself as a jealous God who will visit the iniquities of the fathers upon the children, upon the third and upon the fourth generation of those that hate Him, while yet He shows mercy unto thousands of them that love Him and keep His commandments (Ex. 20:5,6). In the later pages of the Old Testament, psalmists vie with prophets in developing the figure in every detail of its application. Throughout all, the complaint of the Lord is: "Surely as a wife treacherously departeth from her husband, so have ye dealt treacherously with Me, O house of Israel, saith the Lord " (Jer. 3:20). Throughout all, He pleads His changeless though outraged love for them. If He threatens that He will judge them as women that break wedlock are judged, and will bring upon them the blood of fury and jealousy (Ezek. 16:38), He adds: "Nevertheless I will remember My covenant with thee in the days of thy youth, and I will establish unto thee an everlasting covenant. Then shalt thou remember thy ways, and be ashamed . . . when I have forgiven thee all that thou hast done, saith the Lord God" (Ezek. 16:60-63). Throughout all, thus, there throbs the expression of that deep, appropriating love to which punishment is strange work, and which yearns to recover the fallen and restore them to favor and honor. Its hopes run forward in anticipation to that happy day when the wandering one shall listen once again to the alluring words of love spoken to her heart, and once more turn and call the Lord Ishi, "My husband." "And in that day," the Lord hastens to declare, "in that day will I make a covenant for them with the beasts of the field, and with the fowls of heaven, and with the creeping things of the ground: and I will break the bow and the sword and the battle out of the land, and will make them to lie down safely. And I will betroth thee unto Me forever; yea I will betroth thee unto Me in righteousness, and in judgment, and in lovingkindness, and in mercies. I will even betroth thee unto Me in faithfulness: and thou shalt know the Lord" (Hos. 2:18-20).

In its general meaning, thus, our text is general Bible teaching. It announces nothing which had not been the possession of God's people concerning His love for them from the days of old. Its message to us is just the common message of the whole Scripture revelation, in Old and New Testament alike. But it has its own peculiarities in expressing this one great common message of God's yearning love for His people. And possibly there may be found a special lesson for us in these peculiarities.

The first of them which claims our attention is the intense energy of the expression which is used here to declare the love of God for His erring people. He is said to "yearn for us, even unto jealous envy."

Modes of speech sufficiently strong had been employed in the prophets of the Old Testament, in the effort to communicate to men the vehemence of God's grief over their sin and the ardor of His longing to recover them to Himself. The simple attribution of the passion of jealousy to Him one would fancy a representation forcible enough. And this representation is heightened in every conceivable way. Even in Exodus (34:14), we meet it in the strengthened form which declares that the very name of God is Jealous— "for the Lord, whose name is Jealous, is a jealous God"— as if this were the characteristic emotion which expressed His very being. Nahum tells us that "the Lord is a jealous God and avengeth; the Lord avengeth and is full of wrath" (Nah. 1:2). And in Zechariah we read that the Lord is "jealous for Zion with great jealousy, and He is jealous for her with great fury" (Zech. 8:2).

But the language of James has an intensity which rises above all Old Testament precedent. Not only does the verb he uses express the idea of eager longing as strongly as it is possible to express it, but its already strong emphasis is still further enhanced by an adverbial addition which goes beyond all usage. The verb is that which is employed by the Greek translators of the Forty-second Psalm: "As the deer panteth after the water brooks, so panteth my soul after Thee, O God." So, with the thirst of the famishing deer for water— so, says James, does God pant after His people whose minds wander from Him. The adverb is one which often occurs in the classics to express the feeling which one is apt to cherish toward a rival, but it is not the ordinary active word for jealousy which is frequently elsewhere applied to God in the Scriptures, but a term of deeper passion which is never elsewhere applied to God, and which is expressive rather of the envious emotion which tears the soul as it contemplates a rival's success. So, with this sickening envy, says James, God contemplates our dallying with the world and the world's pleasures. He envies the world our love— the love due to Him, pledged to Him, but basely withdrawn from Him and squandered upon the world. The combined expression is, you will see, astonishingly intense. God is represented as panting, yearning, after us, even unto not merely jealousy, but jealous envy. Such vehemence of feeling in God is almost incredible; and some commentators, indeed, refuse to believe that it can be ascribed to Him and declare the anthropomorphism involved to be altogether too extreme.

Let us not, however, refuse the blessed assurance that is given us. It is no doubt hard to believe that God loves us. It is doubtless harder to believe that He loves us with so ardent a love as is here described. But He says that He does. He declares that when we wander from Him and our duty toward Him, He yearns after us and earnestly longs for our return; that He envies the world our love and would fain have it turned back to Himself. What can we do but admiringly cry, "Oh, the breadth and length and height and depth of the love of God which passes knowledge!" There is no language in use among men which is strong enough to portray it. Strain the capacity of words to the utmost and still they fall short of expressing the jealous envy with which He contemplates the love of His people for the world, the yearning desire which possesses Him to turn them back to their duty to Him. It is this inexpressibly precious assurance which the text gives us; let us, without doubting, embrace it with hearty faith.

Another peculiarity of the text lies in the clearness with which it distributes the object of this great love of God into individuals.

When the Scriptures make use of the figure of marriage to reveal God's love to His people, it is commonly His people as a body which they have in mind. It is, in the Old Testament, the "house of Israel" whom Jehovah has chosen to be His wife; in the New Testament, it is the church which is the bride, the Lamb's wife. Individuals, as members in particular of the body of Israel or of the church, partake of its fortunes, share in the love poured out upon it, and contribute by their lives to the foulness of its sin or to the beauty of its holiness. It is only as the members are holy that the church can be that glorious church, not having spot or wrinkle or any such thing, but holy and without blemish, which Christ is to present to Himself at the last day. But, though the individuals thus share in the love and glory of the church, it is the church itself and not the individual which is prevailingly represented as the bride of the Lamb. Only occasionally, in the application of the figure, do the individuals seem to be prominently in mind (Ps. 73:27; Rom. 7:4).

In our present passage, however, the reference is directed to the individual and not to the church as a body. It is the individual Christian who is in covenant vows to God, and who is forgetting these vows, when, in the prosecution of his pleasures, he strives and fights his fellowman, instead of depending on God's love to fulfill all his wants. It is the individual who is warned that he is guilty of spiritual adultery when he permits the least shade of love of the world to enter his heart; and that the cherishing of such love, even in thought, is an act of enmity against God. It is the individual who is assured that God jealously envies the world the love which He gives it, and yearns after the return of His love to Him, the Lord, who "longeth for him even unto jealous envy."

This clear individualization of the great truth which the passage enshrines is surely fraught with a very precious message to us. Not the church merely— we might believe that, knowing ourselves only as unworthy members of what is in ideas a glorious church; not the church merely, but you and I are, each, declared to be covenanted with the Lord in the bonds of this holy and intimate relationship, the recipients of His loving care as His bride, nay, the objects of His changeless and yearning affection. Surely this too is an inexpressibly precious assurance, which we would fain, without doubting, embrace with hearty faith.

A third peculiarity of the text lies in its direct attribution of this appropriating love of God for His chosen ones to God the Holy Spirit.

In this the text is almost unique in the whole range of Scripture. In the Old Testament it is Jehovah, the covenant God, who represents the covenanted union between Israel and Himself under the figure of a marriage. It is Jehovah whose name is Jealous; and whose jealousy burns unto envy as He contemplates the unfaithfulness of Israel. In the New Testament, it is prevailingly Christ, the Lamb, who has taken the Church unto Himself as His bride; and Who loves and cherishes His Church as a husband loves and cherishes his wife. But in our present passage, it is specifically God the Holy Spirit who is represented as the subject of this envious jealousy and this yearning affection. "Or think ye that it is a vain and empty saying of Scripture, that the Spirit which He made to dwell in us yearneth jealously?"

And surely it is a great gain from the point of view of the Christian life to have this explicit revelation of the heart of the indwelling Spirit. What James tells us is that it is God the Holy Spirit, whom God has caused to dwell within us, who is the subject of the unchanging love of God's people, which is expressed in these words of unexampled strength as a yearning after us even to jealous envy. Surely this, too, is an inexpressibly precious assurance which we would fain, without doubting, embrace with hearty faith.

And now let us try to realize, in the simplest possible way, what is involved for us in this precious assurance.

Primarily, then, as we have seen, James makes known to us here the precious fact that the Holy Spirit loves us. It is easy to say that this is so far from being a new fact to which the Christian consciousness is unwonted, that it is necessarily implicated in the fundamental Christian postulate that God is love. As the Godhead is one and cannot be divided, so each Person of the Godhead must be the love that God is. The Father is no more love, and the Son is no more love, than the Spirit is love; and when we confess that God is love, we confess, by necessary implication, that the Holy Spirit, who is God, is Himself love. But it will be far more to the point for us to ask ourselves in all seriousness if we have been in the habit of realizing to ourselves the blessed fact that the Holy Spirit loves us. This does not seem to be a form of gratulation in which Christians are accustomed to felicitate themselves.

Our prayers, our jubilations, thank God; also our hearts, are full of the precious facts that the Father loves us and the Son loves us. "For God so loved the world, that He gave His only begotten Son, that whosoever believeth on Him should not perish, but have eternal life." "Behold what manner of love the Father hath bestowed upon us, that we should be called children of God." "Herein is love, not that we loved God, but that He loved us, and sent His Son to be the propitiation for our sins." "God commendeth His own love toward us, in that, while we were yet sinners, Christ died for us." "God, being rich in mercy, for His great love wherewith He loved us, even when we were dead through our trespasses, quickened us together with Christ." "The love of Christ which passeth knowledge." "Christ also loved you and gave Himself up for us an offering and a sacrifice to God." "Hereby know we love, because He laid down His life for us." "Greater love hath no man than this, that a man lay down his life for his friends." "Who shall separate us from the love of Christ?" (John 3:16; 1 John 3:1; 4:9; Rom. 5:8; Eph. 2:4,5; 3:19; 5:2; 1 John 3:16a; John 15:13; Rom. 8:35a). It is in such texts as these that the Christian soul finds the heavenly manna on which it feeds and grows strong. It is with these glorious truths— that God the Father loves us, that Christ the Savior loves us— that we comfort one another in times of darkness and trial; it is these glorious truths that we whisper to our own souls in their moments of weakness and dismay. We never let them escape us. We dare never let them escape us. For to lose hold of them is to feel the light fade from life and the dense darkness of hopeless agony settle down on the heart.

But do we so constantly remember that the Holy Spirit loves us? Do we comfort ourselves so often and so fully with this great fact? We feel the lift of John's appeal: "Beloved, if God so loved us, we also ought to love one another." We feel the force of Paul's declaration that "the love of Christ constraineth us." But do we feel equally the force of Paul's similar appeal: "Now, I beseech you, brethren, by the love of the Spirit, that you strive together with me in your prayers to God"? Are we equally impelled to a life of single-hearted devotion to God by James' challenge: "Or think ye that it is a vain and empty saying of Scripture, that the Spirit which God hath made to dwell in us yearneth after us even unto jealous envy?" Oh, does it not too often pass over our minds as if it were really a vain and empty saying? The love of the Spirit! The yearning, jealous love of the Holy Spirit for our souls! May it come to mean much to us and be ever in our hearts to strengthen and comfort them.

Doubtless the comparative infrequency with which we meditate upon the love which the Holy Spirit bears to us is due partly to the infrequency with which the love of the Spirit is expressly mentioned in Scripture. It is also, however, due partly, doubtless, to our not habitually connecting in our minds the work of the Holy Spirit in the salvation of men with its motive in His ineffable love for us.

We ascribe to God the Father the plan of salvation; and to God the Son the accomplishment of redemption under that plan; and to God the Holy Spirit the application to the souls of sinners of the redemption procured by the Son. We recognize the necessity of the office work of each Person of the blessed Trinity if souls are to be saved. And, if we face the point now and then, we recognize that each step in the blessed progress of salvation is equally the pure out-flow of the incredible love of God— the striving of the Holy Spirit with the sinner in bringing salvation to fruition in the heart, no less than the humiliation of the Son of God even unto the death of the cross, or the gift by the Father of His only begotten to suffer and die for a lost world. But we are accustomed in our thought of it to con-nect the saving work of the Father and the Son with the love which dictated it. We are accustomed to say to ourselves, with never ceas-ing wonder that "God so loved the world, that He gave His only be-gotten Son," that "Greater love hath no man than this, that a man lay down his life for his friends." And we, perhaps, are not so much ac-customed to connect in thought the saving work of the Holy Spirit with the love which no less dictated it. We are, perhaps, not so much accustomed to say to ourselves that herein is love manifested that the Spirit of all holiness is willing to visit such polluted hearts as ours, and even to dwell in them, to make them His home to work cease-lessly and patiently with them, gradually wooing them— through many groanings and many trials— to slow and tentative efforts toward good; and never leaving them until, through His constant grace, they have been won entirely to put off the old man and put on the new man and to stand new creatures before the face of their Father God and their

Redeemer Christ. Surely herein is love! But we are perhaps too little accustomed to remind ourselves explicitly of it.

Yet what immense riches of comfort and joy this great truth has in it for our souls! Were the work of the application of Christ's redemption to us performed by some mere servant-agent indifferent to us and intent only on perfunctorily fulfilling the task committed to him, we might well tremble for our salvation. We know our hearts. We know how sluggish they are in yielding to the drawings of the Spirit. We know how slow they are to forsake sin; how determined they are to cling to their darling iniquities. Ah, well may James declare that our pleasures have taken up arms and pitched their camps in our members, ready for "war to the knife," as we say, with every good impulse; and Paul, in like manner, that the law in our members arrays itself in war against the new desires implanted in the mind by the Spirit, so that in view of this condition, he is impelled to cry out, "O wretched man that I am, who shall deliver us from the body of this death!" Surely the heart of every one of us has often echoed that cry of natural despair. Were these hearts of ours committed to the molding of One who wrought with us only under a sense of duty and not as upheld by untiring love toward us, what hope of the issue could we cherish? There is no possible deed of ingratitude, opposition, rejection toward the Spirit's work in us of which we have not been guilty. Can we hope that He will bear with us? It is only such love that He cherishes toward us— the model of that love which Paul so sympathetically describes that suffereth long, is not provoked, beareth all things, hopeth all things, believeth all things, endureth all things— that could possibly outlive our shameful disregard and our terrible backsliding. It is only because the Spirit which He hath caused to dwell in us yearneth for us even unto jealous envy, that He is able to continue His gracious work of drawing our souls to God amid the incredible oppositions which we give to His holy work.

And here we must not omit to take particular notice of another aspect of the same great fact as James brings it before us. Observe how he here designates the Spirit, whose great love he has portrayed. It is as the "Spirit whom God has caused to dwell within us." It is He, the indwelling Spirit who, we are told, yearns for us with envious jealousy whenever the world obtains a hold upon our hearts.

God in heaven loves us; and it is because God in heaven loves us that He has given His Son to die for us. Christ on the cross— nay, rather, Christ who once hung on the cross but is now seated at the right hand of God, a Prince and a Savior— loves us; and it is because Christ loves us that He died for us and is now become Head over all things for His Church, that all things may work together for good to those who love Him. But the Spirit in our hearts also loves us; infinite love is above us; infinite love is around us; and, praise be to God! infinite love dwells in us. See how close the love of God is brought to us. It is made to throb in our very hearts; to be shed abroad within us; and to work subtly upon us, drawing us to itself from within.

In the light of this great truth, we may perhaps better understand the meaning of Paul when, depicting the conflict going on within the heart of the newborn man, he declares that the flesh lusts against the Spirit and the Spirit against the flesh, as if the Spirit were part of our very being— the only part of our being which lusts against evil, "that we may not do the things that we would." And again in its light, we may perhaps understand somewhat better that other great passage in which Paul declares that when we pray, the Holy Spirit maketh intercession for us with groanings which cannot be uttered. Our prayers may be feeble because our hatred against sin is weak. But there is One within us who loves us with an imperishable love and hates sin with a perfect hatred; and His groans of longing for our release from the bondage of sin reinforce our weak cries. His unutterable groans for us sinners are the measure of His unutterable love for us sinners.

And let us not fail to gather the full gracious meaning of the word "dwell" here. It is the word to denote permanent habitation in contradistinction from temporary sojourning. God has caused this, the Spirit of love, not to visit our hearts merely, but to abide there; not to tarry there for a season merely, tentatively, as it were, and on trial, but to make His home there, to "settle" there, to establish His permanent dwelling there. "Think ye," asks James, "that it is a vain and empty saying of Scripture that the Spirit which God hath caused to settle permanently in our hearts as His home yearneth after us with jealous envy?"

Ah, when God has covenanted with the soul, it is with no half-heartedness! When He represents Himself as having taken us to Himself as a husband takes a wife in the bonds of a holy covenant, it is no temporary union which He has in mind. He leaves no prudent way of escape open to Himself. With Him, the covenant is forever. He sends the Spirit into our hearts to make His home there. And it is because on His part, the covenant is an eternal covenant, and He takes up His abode within us forever, that, when we treat it with levity and lightly break its bonds, He yearneth after us with jealous envy, and cannot be content until He has won us absolutely back to Himself and has eradicated from our hearts every particle of longing for the world and its sinful pleasures. What a great, what an enheartening truth we have here! God dwells within us, dwells there permanently, and this indwelling God loves us, loves us with such changeless love that even our insults to His love are met by Him only with yearning after us, even unto jealous envy.

How deeply we are touched by the stories which reach us from time to time of the persistent love of a father for a wandering son, or of a brother for a sinful brother, or of a friend for a friend who has fallen into evil courses; of how it follows the reckless sinner into all his wicked associations, enters the saloon with him, the gambling hall, the brothel; argues, pleads, uses kindly violence, seeks every mode of restoration possible with unwearied patience and persistency, is not cast off by curses or by blows, or by any evil entreatment, but pursues with constancy and unfailing tact and tender perseverance its one changeless purpose of rescue. Here is the faint reflection of the Holy Spirit's love for our souls.

See us steeped in the sin of the world; loving evil for evil's sake, hating God and all that God stands for, ever seeking to drain deeper and deeper the cup of our sinful indulgence. The Spirit follows us unwaveringly through all. He is not driven away because we are sinners. He comes to us because, being sinners, we need Him. He is not cast off because we reject His loving offices. He abides with us because our rejection of Him would leave us helpless. He does not condition His further help upon our recognizing and returning His love. His continuance with us is conditioned only on His own love for us. And that love for us is so strong, so mighty, and so constant that it can never fail. When He sees us immersed in sin and rushing headlong to destruction, He does not turn from us; He yearns for us with jealous envy.

It is in the hands of such love that we have fallen. And it is because we have fallen into the hands of such love that we have before us a future of eternal hope. When we lose hope in ourselves, when the present becomes dark and the future black before us, when effort after effort has issued only in disheartening failure, and our sin looms big before our despairing eyes; when our hearts hate and despise themselves, and we remember that God is greater than our hearts and cannot abide the least iniquity; the Spirit whom He has sent to bring us to Him still labors with us, not in indifference or hatred, but in pitying love. Yea, His love burns all the stronger because we so deeply need His help: *He is yearning after us with jealous envy.*

Among the legends which popular fancy has woven around the memory of Francis of Assisi, we are told that he was riding along one day in the first joy of his new-found peace, his mind possessed with a desire to live over again the life of absolute love which his divine Master had lived in the earth. Suddenly, "at a turn in the road, he found himself face to face with a leper. The frightful malady had always inspired in him an invincible repulsion. He could not control a movement of horror, and by instinct he turned his horse in another direction." Then came the quick revulsion of feeling. "He retraced his steps and, springing from his horse, he gave to the astounded sufferer all the money that he had; and then kissed his hand, as he would have done to a priest." A new era in his spiritual life had dawned. He visited the lazaretto itself and, with largesses of alms and kindly words, sought to bring some brightness of the outside world into that gloomy retreat. Still his love grew stronger. The day came when he made the great renunciation and stood before men endued with naught but the love of Christ. Now no temporary lazaretto contented him. He must dwell there as a permanent sunbeam to the distressed. He came now with empty hands, but with a heart full to overflowing with compassion. "Taking up his abode in the midst of the afflicted, he lavished upon them a most touching care, washing and wiping their sores, all the more gentle and radiant as the sores were more repulsive."

It is not given to man, of course, even to comprehend, much less to embody in a legend like this, all the richness of God's mysterious love for sinners. But in such legends as this, we may catch some faint shadow of what the Spirit's love for us means. No leprous sores can be as foul in the eyes of the daintiest bred as sin is foul in the eyes of the Holy Spirit. We cannot conceive of the energy of

His shrinking from its polluting touch. Yet He comes into the foul lazaretto of our hearts and dwells there— permanently lives there; not for Himself, or for any good to accrue to Himself, but solely that He may cleanse us and fit us to be what He has made us, the Bride, the Lamb's wife.

Could there be presented to us a more complete manifestation of the infinite love of God than is contained in this revelation of the love of the Spirit for us? God is love. Does not this greatest of all revelations take on a new brightness and a new force to move our souls when we come to realize that not only is the Father love, and the Son love, but the Spirit also is love; and so wholly love that, despite the foulness of our sin, He yearneth for us even unto jealous envy?

Could there be given us a higher incentive to faithfulness to God than is contained in this revelation of the love of the Spirit for us? Are our hearts so hard that they are incapable of responding to the appeal of such a love as this? Can we dally with the world, seek our own pleasures, forget our duty of love to God, when the Spirit which He hath made to dwell in us is yearning after us even unto jealous envy?

Could there be afforded us a deeper ground of encouragement in our Christian life than is contained in this revelation of the love of the Spirit for us? Is hope so dead within us that it is no longer possible for us to rest with confidence upon such love? Can we doubt what the end shall be— despite all that the world can do to destroy us, and the flesh and the devil— when we know that the Spirit which He hath made to dwell in us is yearning after us even unto jealous envy?

Could there, then, be granted us a firmer foundation for the holy joy of Christian assurance than is contained in this revelation of the love of the Spirit for us? Is faith grown so weak that it cannot stay itself on the almighty arm of God? Surely, surely, though our hearts faint within us, and the way seems dark, and there are lions roaring in the path, we shall be able to look past them all to the open gates of pearl beyond, whenever we remember that the Spirit which He hath made to dwell within us is yearning after us even unto jealous envy!

ARTICLES

13

THE SPIRIT OF GOD IN THE OLD TESTAMENT

(from the Shorter Writings, Vol. II)

In passing from the Old Testament to the New, the reader is conscious of no violent discontinuity in the conception of the Spirit which he finds in the two volumes. He may note the increased frequency with which the name appears on the printed page. But he would note this much the same in passing from the earlier to the later chapters of the Epistle to the Romans. He may note an increased definiteness and fullness in the conception itself. But something similar to this he would note in passing from the Pentateuch to Isaiah, or from Matthew to John or Paul. The late Professor Smeaton[8] may have overstated the matter in his interesting Cunningham Lectures on *The Doctrine of the Holy Spirit*. "We find," he says, "that the doctrine of the Spirit taught by the Baptist, by Christ, and by the apostles, was in every respect the same as that with which the Old Testament church was familiar. We nowhere find that their Jewish hearers took exception to it. The teaching of our Lord and His apostles never called forth a question or an opposition from any quarter— a plain proof that on this question nothing was taught by them which came into collision with the sentiments and opinions which, up to that time, had been accepted, and still continued to be current among the Jews."[9] But if there be any fundamental difference between the Old and the New Testament conceptions of the Spirit of God, it escapes us in our ordinary reading of the Bible, and we naturally and without conscious straining read our New Testament conceptions into the Old Testament passages.

We are, indeed, bidden to do this by the New Testament itself. The New Testament writers identify their "Holy Spirit" with the "Spirit of God" of the older books. All that is attributed to the Spirit of God in the Old Testament is attributed by them to their personal Holy Spirit. It was their own Holy Spirit who was Israel's guide and director and whom Israel rejected when they resisted the leading of God (Acts 7:51). It was in Him that Christ (doubtless in the person of Noah) preached to the antediluvians [10](1 Peter 3:18). It was He who was the author of faith of old as well as now (2 Cor. 4:13). It was He who gave Israel its ritual service (Heb. 9:8). It was He who spoke in and through David and Isaiah and all the prophets (Matt. 22:43; Mark 12:36; Acts 1:16; 28:25; Heb. 3:7; 10:15). If Zechariah (7:12) or Nehemiah (9:20) tells us that Jehovah of Hosts sent His word by His Spirit by the hands of the prophets, Peter tells us that these men from God were moved by the Holy Spirit to speak these words (2 Pet. 1:21), and even that it was specifically the Spirit of Christ that was in the prophets (1 Pet. 1:11). We are assured that it was in Christ, upon whom the Holy Spirit had visibly descended, that Isaiah's predictions were fulfilled that Jehovah would put His Spirit upon His righteous servant (Isa. 42:1) and that the Spirit of the Lord Jehovah should be upon Him (Isa. 61:1; Matt. 12:18; Luke 4:18,19). And Peter bids us look upon the descent of the Holy Spirit at Pentecost as the accomplished promise of Joel that God would pour out His Spirit upon all flesh (Joel 2:27,28; Acts 2:17). There can be no doubt that the New Testament writers identify the Holy Spirit of the New Testament with the Spirit of God of the Old.

This fact, of course, abundantly justifies the instinctive Christian identification. We are sure, with the surety of a divine revelation, that the Spirit of God of the Old Testament is the personal Holy Spirit of the New. But this assurance does not forestall the inquiry whether this personal Spirit was so fully revealed in the Old Testament that those who were dependent on that revelation alone, without the inspired commentary of the New, were able to know Him as He is known to us who enjoy fuller light. Whether this be so, or, if so in some measure, how far it may be true is a matter of separate investigation. The Spirit of God certainly acts as a person, throughout the

Old Testament. In no passage is He conceived otherwise than personally— as a free, willing, intelligent being. This is, however, in itself only the pervasive testimony of the Scriptures to the personality of God. For it is equally true that the Spirit of God is everywhere in the Old Testament identified with God. This is only its pervasive testimony to the divine unity. The question for examination is, how far the one personal God was conceived of as embracing in His unity hypostatical distinctions.[11] This question is a very complicated one and needs very delicate treatment. There are, indeed, three questions included in the general one, which for the sake of clearness we ought to keep apart. We may ask, "May the Christian properly see in the Spirit of God of the Old Testament the personal Holy Spirit of the New?" This we may answer at once in the affirmative. We may ask again, "Are there any hints in the Old Testament anticipating and adumbrating the revelation of the hypostatic Spirit of the New?" This also, it seems, we ought to answer in the affirmative. We may ask again, "Are these hints of such clearness as actually to reveal this doctrine, apart from the revelation of the New Testament?" This should be doubtless answered in the negative. There are hints and they serve for points of attachment for the fuller New Testament teaching. But they are only hints, and, apart from the New Testament teaching, would be readily explained as personifications, or ideal objectivations of the power of God.

Undoubtedly, side by side with the stress put upon the unity of God and the identity of the Spirit with the God who gives it, there is a distinction recognized between God and His Spirit— in the sense at least of a discrimination between God over all and God in all, between the Giver and the Given, between the Source and the Executor of the moral law. This distinction already emerges in Genesis 1:2; and it does not grow less observable as we advance through the Old Testament. It is prominent in the standing phrases by which, on the one hand, God is spoken of as sending, putting, placing, pouring, emptying His Spirit upon man, and on the other the Spirit is spoken of as coming, resting, falling, springing upon man. There is a sort of objectifying of the Spirit over against God in both cases; in the former case, by sending Him from Himself God, as it were, separates Him from Himself; in the latter, the Spirit appears almost as a distinct person, acting *sua sponte*.[12] Schultz does not hesitate to speak of the

Spirit even in Genesis 1:2 as appearing "as very independent, just like a hypostatis or person." Kleinert finds in this passage at least a tendency toward hypostatizing— though he thinks this tendency was not subsequently worked out. Perhaps we are warranted in saying as much as that: that there is observable in the Old Testament, not, indeed, a hypostatizing of the Spirit of God, but *a tendency* toward it— that, in Hofmann's cautious language, the Spirit appears in the Old Testament "as a 'somewhat' distinct from the 'I' of God which God makes the principle of life in the world." A preparation, at least, for the full revelation of the Trinity in the New Testament is observable; points of connection with it are discoverable: and thus Christians are able to read the Old Testament without offense and to find without confusion their own Holy Spirit in its Spirit of God.

More than this could scarcely be looked for. The elements in the doctrine of God which above others needed emphasis in the Old Testament times, were naturally His *unity* and His *personality*. The great things to be taught the ancient people of God was that the God of all the earth is one person. Over against the varying idolatries about them, this was the truth of truths for which Israel was primarily to stand; and not until this great truth was ineffaceably stamped upon their souls could the personal distinctions in the Triune God be safely made known to them. A premature revelation of the Spirit as a distinct hypostasis could have wrought nothing but harm to the people of God. We shall all, no doubt, agree with Kleinert that it is pragmatic in Isidore of Pelusium[13] to say that Moses knew the doctrine of the Trinity well enough, but concealed it through fear that polytheism would profit by it. But we may safely affirm this of God the Revealer, in the gradual delivery of the truth concerning Himself to men. He reveals the whole truth, but in divers portions and in divers manners; and it was incident to the progressive delivery of doctrine that the unity of the Godhead should first be made the firm possession of men, and the Trinity in that unity should be conveyed to them only afterward, when the times were ripe for it. What we need wonder over is not that the hypostatical distinctness of the Spirit is not more clearly revealed in the Old Testament, but that the approaches to it are laid so skillfully that the doctrine of the hypostatical Holy Spirit of the New Testament finds so many and such striking points of attachment in the Old Testament, and yet no Israelite had ever been disturbed in repeating with hearty faith his great *Shema*,[14] "Hear, O Israel, the Lord our God is one Lord" (Deut. 6:4). Not until the whole doctrine of the Trinity was ready to be manifested in such visible form as at the baptism of Christ— God in heaven, God on earth, and God descending from heaven to earth— could any part of the mystery be safely uncovered.

The temporary withholding of exact information as to the relation of the Spirit of God to the Godhead did not prevent, however, a very rich revelation to the Old Testament saints of the operations of the Spirit of God in the world, in the Church and in the individual soul. Least of all could it prevent the performance by the Spirit of His several functions in the world, in the Church, and in the soul throughout the whole Old Testament dispensation. That too was a dispensation in which the Spirit of God wrought. What then is meant by calling the new dispensation the dispensation of the Spirit? What does John mean by saying that the Spirit was not yet given (John 7:39) because Jesus was not yet glorified? What our Lord Himself, when He promised the Comforter, by saying that the Comforter would not come until He went away and sent Him (John 16:7); and by breathing on His disciples, saying, "Receive the Holy Spirit" (John 20:22)? What did the descent of the Spirit at Pentecost mean, when He came to inaugurate the dispensation of the Spirit? It cannot be meant that the Spirit was not active in the old dispensation. We have already seen that the New Testament writers themselves represent Him to have been active in the old dispensation in all the varieties of activity with which He is active in the new. Such passages seem to have diverse references. Some of them may refer to the specifically miraculous endowments which characterized the apostles and the churches which they founded. Others refer to the worldwide mission of the Spirit, promised, indeed, in the Old Testament, but only now to be realized. But there is a more fundamental idea to be reckoned with still. This is the idea of the *preparatory nature* of the Old Testament dispensation.[15]

The old dispensation was a preparatory one and must be strictly conceived as such. What spiritual blessings came to it were by way of prelibation. They were many and various. The Spirit worked in providence no less universally then than now. He abode in the Church not less really then than now. He wrought in the hearts of God's people not less prevalently then than now. All the good that was in the world was then as now due to Him. All the hope of God's Church then as now depended on Him. Every grace of the godly life then as now was a fruit of His working. But the object of the whole dispensation was only *to prepare* for the outpouring of the Spirit upon all flesh. He kept the remnant safe and pure, but it was in order that the seed might be preserved. This was the end of His activity, then. The dispensation of the Spirit, properly so-called, did not dawn, however, until the period of preparation was over and the day of outpouring had come. The mustard seed had been preserved through all the ages only by the Spirit's brooding care. Now it is planted, and it is by His operation that it is growing up into a great tree which shades the whole earth, and to the branches of which all the fowls of heaven come for shelter. It is not that the work is more real in the new dispensation than in the old. It is not merely that it is more universal. It is that it is directed to a different end— that it is no longer for the mere preserving of the seed unto the day of planting, but for the perfecting of the fruitage and the gathering of the harvest. The Church, to use a figure of Isaiah's, was then like a pent-in stream;[16] it is now like that pent-in stream with the barriers broken down and the Spirit of the Lord driving it. It was He who preserved it in being when it was pent-in. It is He who is now driving on its gathered floods till it shall cover the earth as the waters cover the sea. In one word, that was a day in which the Spirit restrained His power. Now the great day of the Spirit is come!

14

THE SPIRIT OF GOD IN THE OLD TESTAMENT

(from Biblical & Theological Studies[17])

The doctrine of the Spirit of God is an exclusively Biblical doctrine. Ruckert[18] tells us that the idea connoted by the term is entirely foreign to Hellenism,[19] and first came into the world through Christianity. And Kleinert,[20] in quoting this remark, adds that what is peculiarly anti-heathenish in the conception is already present in the Old Testament. It would seem, then, that what is most fundamental in the Biblical doctrine of the Spirit of God is common to both Testaments.

The name meets us in the very opening verses of the Old Testament, and it appears there as unannounced and unexplained as in the opening verses of the New Testament. It is plain that it was no more a novelty in the mouth of the author of Genesis than in the mouth of the author of Matthew. But though it is common to both Testaments, it is not equally common in all parts of the Bible. It does not occur as frequently in the Old Testament as in the New. It is found as often in the Epistles of Paul as in the whole Old Testament. It is not as pervasive in the Old Testament as in the New. It fails in no New Testament book, except the three brief personal letters Philemon and 2 and 3 John. On the other hand, in only some half of the thirty-nine Old Testament books is it clearly mentioned,[21] while in an many as sixteen all definite allusion to it seems to be lacking.[22] The principle which governs the use or disuse of it does not lie on the surface. Sometimes it may, perhaps, be partly due to the nature of the subject treated. But if mention of the Spirit of God fails in Leviticus, it is made in Numbers; if it fails in Joshua and Ruth, it is made in Judges and Samuel; if it fails in Ezra, it is made in Nehemiah; if it fails in Jeremiah, it is made in Isaiah and Ezekiel; if it fails in seven or eight of the minor prophets, it is made in the remaining four or five. Whether it occurs in an Old Testament book seems to depend on a number of circumstances which have little or no bearing on the history of the doctrine. We need only note that the name "Spirit of God" meets us at the very opening of revelation, and it, or its equivalents, accompanies us sporadically throughout the volume. The Pentateuch and historical books provide us with the outline of the doctrine; its richest depositories among the prophets are Isaiah and Ezekiel, from each of which alone probably the whole doctrine could be derived.[23]

In passing from the Old Testament to the New, the reader is conscious of no violent discontinuity in the conception of the Spirit which he finds in the two volumes. He may note the increased frequency with which the name appears on the printed page. But he would note this much the same in passing from the earlier to the later chapters of the *Epistle to the Romans*. He may note an increased definiteness and fullness in the conception itself. But something similar to this he would note in passing from the Pentateuch to Isaiah, or from Matthew to John or Paul. The late Professor Smeaton may have overstated the matter in his interesting Cunningham Lectures on "The Doctrine of the Holy Spirit." "We find," he says, "that the doctrine of the Spirit taught by the Baptist, by Christ and by the Apostles, was in every respect the same as that with which the Old Testament church was familiar. We nowhere find that their Jewish hearers on any occasion took exception to it. The teaching of our Lord and His Apostles never called forth a question or an opposition from any quarter— a plain proof that on this question nothing was taught by them which came into collision with the sentiments and opinions which up to that time had been accepted, and still continued to be current among the Jews." Some such change in the conception of God doubtless needs to be recognized as that which Dr. Denney describes in the following words: "The Apostles were all Jews,— men, as it has been said, with monotheism as a passion in their blood.[24] They did not cease to be monotheists when they became preachers of Christ, but they instinctively conceived God in a way in which the old revelation had not taught them to conceive him. . . . Distinctions were recognized in what had once been the bare simplicity of the divine nature. The distinction of Father and Son was the most obvious, and it was enriched, on the basis of Christ's own teaching, and of the actual experience of the Church, by the further distinction of the Holy Spirit."[25] But if there be any fundamental difference between the Old and the New Testament conceptions of the Spirit of God, it escapes us in our ordinary reading of the Bible, and we naturally and without conscious straining read our New Testament conceptions into the Old Testament passages.

We are, indeed, bidden to do this by the New Testament itself. The New Testament writers identify their "Holy Spirit" with the "Spirit of God" of the older books. All that is attributed to the Spirit of God in the Old Testament, is attributed by them to their personal Holy Spirit. It was their own Holy Spirit who was Israel's guide and director and whom Israel rejected when they resisted the leading of God (Acts 7:51). It was in Him that Christ (doubtless in the person of Noah) preached to the antediluvians (1 Pet. 3:18). It was He who was the author of faith of old as well as now (2 Cor. 4:13). It was He who gave Israel its ritual service (Heb 9:8). It was He who spoke in and through David and Isaiah and all the prophets (Matt. 22:43; Mark 12:36; Acts 1:16, 28:25; Heb. 3:7, 10:15). If Zechariah (7:12) or Nehemiah (9:20) tells us that Jehovah of Hosts sent His word by His Spirit by the hands of the prophets, Peter tells us that these men from God were moved by the Holy Spirit to speak these words (2 Pet 1:21), and even that it was specifically the Spirit of Christ that was in the prophets (1 Pet. 1:11). We are assured that it was in Jesus upon whom the Holy Spirit had visibly descended, that Isaiah's predictions were fulfilled that Jehovah would put His Spirit upon his righteous servant (Isa. 42:1) and that (Isa. 61:1) the Spirit of the Lord Jehovah should be upon Him (Matt. 12:18; Luke 4:18, 19). And Peter bids us look upon the descent of the Holy Spirit at Pentecost as the accomplished promise of Joel that God would pour out His Spirit upon all flesh (Joel 2:27, 28; Acts 2:16).[26] There can be no doubt that the New Testament writers identify the Holy Spirit of the New Testament with the Spirit of God of the Old.

This fact, of course, abundantly justifies the instinctive Christian identification. We are sure, with the surety of a divine revelation, that the Spirit of God of the Old Testament is the personal Holy Spirit of the New. But this assurance does not forestall the inquiry whether this personal Spirit was so fully revealed in the Old Testament that those who were dependent on that revelation alone, without the inspired commentary of the New, were able to know Him as He is known to us who enjoy the fuller light. The principle of the progressive delivery of doctrine in the age-long process of God's self-revelation, is not only a reasonable one in itself and one which is justified by the results of investigation, but it is one which is assumed in the Scriptures themselves as God's method of revealing Himself, and which received the practical endorsement of our Savior in His manner of communicating His saving truth to men. The question is still an open one, therefore, how much of the doctrine of the Holy Spirit as it lies in its completeness in the pages of the New Testament had already been made the property of the men of the old dispensation; in other words, what the Old Testament doctrine of the Spirit of God is. We may not find this inconsistent with the fuller New Testament teaching, but we may find it fall short of the whole truth revealed in the latter days in God's Son.

The deep unity between the New and Old Testament conceptions lies, in one broad circumstance, so upon the surface of the two Testaments that our attention is attracted to it at the outset of any investigation of the material. In both Testaments the Spirit of God appears distinctly as *the executive of the Godhead*. If in the New Testament God works all that He does by the Spirit, so in the Old Testament the Spirit is the name of God working. The Spirit of God is in the Old Testament the executive name of God— "the divine principle of activity everywhere at work in the world."[27] In this common conception lies doubtless the primary reason why we pass from one Testament to the other without sense of discontinuity in the doctrine of the Spirit. The further extent in which this unity may be traced will depend on the nature of the activities which are ascribed to the Spirit in both Testaments.

The Old Testament does not give us, of course, an exhaustive record of all God's activities. It is primarily an account of God's redemptive work prior to the coming of the Messiah— of the progress, in a word, so far, of the new creation of grace built upon the ruins of the first creation, a short account of which is prefixed as background and basis. In the nature of the case, we learn from the Old Testament of those activities of God only which naturally emerge in these accounts; and accordingly the doctrine of the Spirit of God as the divine principle of activity, as taught in the Old Testament, is necessarily confined to the course of divine activities in the first and the initial stages of the second creation. In other words, it is subsumable under the two broad captions of God in the world, and God in His people. It is from this that the circumstance arises which has been frequently noted, that, after the entrance of sin into the world, the work of the Spirit of God on men's spirits is always set forth in the Old Testament in the interests and in the spirit of the kingdom of God.[28] The Old Testament is concerned after the sin of man only with the recovery of man; it traces the preparatory stages of the kingdom of God, as God laid its foundations in a chosen nation in whom all the nations of the earth were to be blessed. The segregation of Israel and the establishment of the theocracy thus mark the first steps in the new creation; and following this course of divine working, the doctrine of the Spirit in the new creation as taught in the Old Testament naturally concerns especially the activities of God in the establishment and development of the theocracy and in the preparation of a people to enjoy its blessings. In other words, it falls under the two captions of His national, or rather churchly, and of His individual work. Thus the Old Testament teaching concerning the Spirit, brings before us three spheres of His activity, which will correspond broadly to the conceptions of God in the world, God in the theocracy, and God in the soul.

Broadly speaking, these three spheres of the Spirit's activity appear successively in the pages of the Old Testament. In these pages the Spirit of God is introduced to us primarily in His cosmical, next in His theocratic, and lastly in His individual relations.[29] This is, of course, due chiefly to the natural correspondence of the aspects of His activity which are presented with the course of history, and is not to be taken so strictly as to imply that the revelations relative to each sphere of His working occur exclusively in a single portion of the Old Testament. It supplies us, however, not only with the broad outlines of the historical development of the doctrine of the Spirit in the Old Testament, but also with a logical order of presentation for the material. Perhaps we may also say, in passing, that it suggests a course of development of the doctrine of the Spirit which is at once most natural and, indeed, rationally inevitable, and, as Dr. Dale points out,[30] closely correspondent with what have come to be spoken of as the "traditional" dates attributed to the books of the Old Testament. These books, standing as they stand in this dating, are in the most natural order for the development of this doctrine.

THE COSMICAL SPIRIT

I. The Spirit of God is first brought before us in the Old Testament, then, in His relations to the first creation, or in what may be called His cosmical relations. In this connection He is represented as the source of all order, life and light in the universe. He is the divine principle of all movement, of all life and of all thought in the world. The basis of this conception is already firmly laid in the first passage in which the Spirit of God is mentioned (Gen. 1:2). In the beginning, we are told, God created the heavens and the earth. And then the process is detailed by which the created earth, at first waste and void, with darkness resting upon the face of the deep, was transformed by successive fiats into the ordered and populous world in which we live. As the ground of the whole process, we are informed that "the Spirit of God was brooding upon the face of the waters," as much as to say that the obedience, and the precedent power of obedience, of the waste of waters to the successive creative words— as God said, "Let there be light; Let there be a firmament; Let the waters be gathered together; Let the waters and the earth bring forth"— depended upon the fact that the Spirit of God was already brooding upon the formless void. To the voice of God in heaven saying, "Let there be light!" the energy of the Spirit of God brooding upon the face of the waters responded, and lo! there was light. Over against the transcendent God, above creation, there seems to be postulated here God brooding upon creation, and the suggestion seems to be that it is only by virtue of God brooding upon creation that the created thing moves and acts and works out the will of God. The Spirit of God, in a word, appears at the very opening of the Bible as God immanent; and, as such, is set over against God transcendent. And it is certainly very instructive to observe that God is conceived as immanent already in what may be called the formless world-stuff which by His immanence in it alone it constituted a stuff from which on the divine command an ordered world may emerge.[31] The Spirit of God thus appears from the outset of the Old Testament as the principle of the very existence and persistence of all things, and as the source and originating cause of all movement and order and life. God's thought and will and word take effect in the world, because God is not only over the world, thinking and willing and commanding, but also in the world, as the principle of all activity, *executing*: this seems the thought of the author of the Biblical cosmogony.[32]

A series of Old Testament passages range themselves under this conception and carry it forward. It is by the Spirit of God, says Job, that the heavens are garnished (26:13). Isaiah compares the coming of the God of vengeance, repaying fury to His adversaries and recompense to His enemies, to the bursting forth "of a pent-in stream which the Spirit of Jehovah driveth" (59:19); and represents the perishing of flesh as like the withering of the grass and the fading of the flower when "the Spirit of Jehovah bloweth upon it" (40:7). In such passages the Spirit appears as the principle of cosmical processes. He is also the source of all life, and, as such, the executor of Him with whom, as the Psalmist says, is the fountain of life (Ps. 36:9). The Psalmist accordingly ascribes the being of all creatures to Him: "Thou sendest forth thy Spirit, they are created" (Ps 104:30). "The Spirit of God hath made me," declares Job, "and the breath of the Almighty giveth me life" (33:4). Accordingly he represents life to be due to the persistence of the Spirit of God in his nostrils (27:3), and therefore its continuance to be dependent upon the continuance of the Spirit with man: "If He set His heart upon man, if He gather unto Himself His Spirit and His breath all flesh shall perish together, and man shall turn again unto dust" (34:14,15; cf. 12:10). He is also the source of all intellectual life. Elihu tells us that it is not greatness, nor years, but the Spirit of God that gives understanding: "There is a Spirit in man, and the breath of the Almighty giveth them understanding" (Job 32:8)— a thought which is probably only expressed in another way in Prov. 20:27, which declares that the spirit of man is "the lamp of the Lord, searching all the innermost parts of the belly." That the Spirit is the source also of all ethical life seems to follow from the obscure passage, Genesis 6:3: "And the Lord said, My Spirit shall not strive with man for ever, for that he also is flesh." Apparently there is here either a direct threat from Jehovah to withdraw that Spirit by virtue of which alone morality could exist in the world, or else a threat that He will, on account of their sin, withdraw the Spirit whose presence gives life so that men may no longer be upheld in their wicked existence, but may sink back into nothingness. In either case ethical considerations come forward prominently,— the occasion of the destruction of mankind is an ethical one, and the gift of life appears as for ethical ends. This, however, is an element in the conception of the Spirit's work which comes to clear enunciation only in another connection.

It would not be easy to overestimate the importance of the early emergence of this doctrine of the immanent Spirit of God, side by side with the high doctrine of the transcendence of God which pervades the Old Testament. Whatever tendency the emphasis on the transcendence of God might engender toward Deistic conceptions would be corrected at once by such teaching as to the immanent Spirit; while in turn any tendencies to Pantheistic[33] or Cosmotheistic[34] conceptions which it might itself arouse would be corrected not only by the prevailing stress upon the divine transcendence, but also by the manner in which the immanence of God is itself presented. For we cannot sufficiently admire the perfection with which, in delivering the doctrine of the immanent Spirit, all possibility is excluded of conceiving of God as entangled in creation— as if the Spirit of God were merely the physical world-spirit, the proper ground rather than effecting cause of cosmical activities. In the very phraseology of Genesis 1:2, for example, the moving Spirit is kept separate from the matter to which He gives movement; He *broods over* rather than is merged in the waste of waters; He acts upon them and cannot be confounded with them as but another name for their own blind surging. So in the 104th Psalm (verses 29, 30) the creative Spirit is *sent forth* by God, and is not merely an alternative name for the unconscious life-ground of nature. It is a thing which is *given* by God and so produces life (Isa. 42:5). Though penetrating all things (Ps. 139:7) and the immanent source of all life-activities (Ps. 104:30), it is nevertheless always the *personal* cause of physical, psychical and ethical activities. It exercises choice. It is not merely the *general* ground of all such activities; it is the determiner as well of all the *differences* that exist among men. so, for example, Elihu appeals to the Spirit of understanding that is in him (Job 32:8). It is not merely the ground of the *presence* of these powers; it is also to it that their *withdrawal* is to be ascribed (Isa. 40:7, Gen. 6:3). Nor are its manifestations confined altogether to what may be called *natural* modes of action; room is left among them for what we may call truly *supernatural* activity (1 Kgs. 18:12, 2 Kgs. 2:16, cf. 2 Kgs. 19:7, Isa. 37:7). All nature worship is further excluded by the clearness of the identification of the Spirit of God with the God over all. Thus the unity of God was not only preserved but emphasized, and men were taught to look upon the emergence of divine powers and effects in nature as the work of His hands. "Whither shall I go," asks the Psalmist, "from thy Spirit? or whither shall I flee from thy presence" (Ps. 139:7)? Here the spiritual presence of God is obviously the presence of the God over all in His Spirit. "Who hath . . . meted out heaven with a span? . . . Who hath meted out the Spirit of Jehovah, or being his counselor hath taught him?" asks Isaiah (40:12, 13) in the same spirit. Obviously the Spirit of God was not conceived as the impersonal ground of life and understanding, but as the personal source of all that was of being, life and light in the world, not as apart from but as one with the great God almighty in the heavens. And yet, as immanent in the world, He is set over against God transcendent in a manner which prepares the way for His hypostatizing and so for the Christian doctrine of the Trinity.

It requires little consideration to realize how greatly the Old Testament conception of God is enriched by this teaching. In particular, it behooves us to note how, side by side with the emphasis that is laid upon God as the maker of all things, this doctrine lays an equal emphasis on God as the upholder and governor of all things. Side by side with the emphasis which is laid on the unapproachable majesty of God as the transcendent Person, it lays an equal emphasis on God as the immanent agent in all world changes and all world movements. It thus lays firmly the foundation of the Christian doctrine of Providence— God in the world and in history, leading all things to their destined goal. If without God there was not anything made that has been made, so without God's Spirit there has not anything occurred that has occurred.

The Holy Spirit

THE THEOCRATIC SPIRIT

II. All this is still further emphasized in the second and predominant aspect in which the Spirit of God is brought before us in the Old Testament, viz., in His relations to the second creation.

(1) Here, primarily, He is presented as the source of all the supernatural powers and activities which are directed to the foundation and preservation and development of the kingdom of God in the midst of the wicked world. He is thus represented as the theocratic Spirit as pointedly as He is represented as the world-spirit. We are moving here in a distinctly supernatural atmosphere and the activities which come under review belong to an entirely supernatural order. There are a great variety of these activities, but they have this in common: they are all endowments of the theocratic organs with the gifts requisite for the fulfillment of their functions.[35]

There are, for example, the supernatural gifts of strength, resolution, energy, courage in battle which were awakened in chosen leaders for the service of God's people. Thus we are told that the Spirit of Jehovah came upon Othniel to fit him for his work as judge of Israel (Judg. 3:10), and clothed itself with Gideon (6:34), and came upon Jephthah (11:29), and, most remarkably of all, came mightily upon and moved Samson, endowing him with superhuman strength (13:25, 14:6, 19, 15:14). Similarly the Spirit of God came mightily upon Saul (1 Sam. 11:6) and upon David (1 Sam. 16:13), and clothed Amasai (1 Chron. 12:18). Then, there are the supernatural gifts of skill by which artificers were fitted to serve the kingdom of God in preparing a worthy sanctuary for the worship of the King. There were, for instance, those whom Jehovah had filled with the spirit of wisdom and who were, therefore, wise-hearted to make Aaron's sacred garments (Ex. 28:3). And especially we are told that Jehovah had filled Bezalel "with the Spirit of God, in wisdom and in understanding, and in knowledge, and in all manner of workmanship, to devise cunning works, to work in gold, and in silver, and in brass, and in cutting of stones for setting, and in carving of wood, to work in all manner of workmanship" (Ex. 31:3f. cf. 35:31)— and that he should therefore preside over the work of the wise-hearted, in whom the Lord had put wisdom, for the making of the tabernacle and its furniture. Similarly when the temple came to be built, the pattern of it, we are told, was

128

given of Jehovah "by His Spirit" to David (1 Chron. 28:12). Quite near to these gifts, but on a higher plane, lies the supernatural gift of wisdom for the administration of judgment and government. Moses was so endowed. And, therefore, the seventy elders were also endowed with it, to fit them to share his cares: "And I will take of the Spirit which is upon thee," said Jehovah, "and will put it upon them; and they shall bear the burden of the people with thee" (Num. 11:17, 25).[36] It is in this sense also, doubtless, that Joshua is said to have been full of the Spirit of wisdom (Num. 27:18, Deut. 34:9).[37] In these aspects, the gift of the Spirit, appearing as it does as an endowment for office, is sometimes sacramentally connected with symbols of conference: in the case of Joshua with the laying on of hands (Deut. 34:9), in the cases of Saul and David with anointing (1 Sam. 10:1, 16:13). Possibly its symbolical connection in Samson's case with Nazaritic length of hair may be classed in the same general category.

Prominent above all other theocratic gifts of the Spirit, however, are the gifts of supernatural knowledge and insight, culminating in the great gift of Prophecy. This greatest of gifts in the service of the Kingdom of God is sometimes very closely connected with the other gifts which have been mentioned. Thus the presence of the Spirit in the seventy elders in the wilderness, endowing them to share the burden of judgment with Moses, was manifested by prophetic utterance (Num. 11:25). The descent of the Spirit upon Saul was likewise manifested by his prophesying (1 Sam. 10:6, 10). Sometimes the Spirit's presence in the prophet even manifest itself in the production in others of what may be called sympathetic prophecy accompanied with ecstasy. Instances occur in the cases of the messengers sent by Saul and of Saul himself, when they went to apprehend David (1 Sam. 19:20, 23); and in these cases the phenomenon served the ulterior purpose of a protection for the prophets.[38] In the visions of Ezekiel the presence of the inspiring Spirit is manifested in physical as well as in mental effects (Ezek. 3:12, 14, 24, 8:3, 11:1, 5, 24, 37:1). Thus clear it is that all these are the work of one and the same Spirit.

In all cases, however, Prophecy is the free gift of the Spirit of God to special organs chosen for the purpose of the revelation of His will. It is so represented in the cases of Balaam (Num. 24:2), of Saul (1 Sam. 10:6), of David (1 Sam. 16:13), of Azariah the son of Oded (2 Chron. 15:1), of Jahaziel the son of Zechariah (2 Chron. 20:14), of

Zechariah the son of Jehoiada (2 Chron. 24:20). To Hosea, "the man that hath the Spirit" was a synonym for "prophet" (9:7). Isaiah (48:16) in a somewhat puzzling sentence declares, "The Lord God hath sent me and His Spirit," which seems to conjoin the Spirit either with Jehovah as the source of the mission, or else with the prophet as the bearer of the message; and, in either case, refers the prophetic inspiration to the Spirit. A very full insight into the nature of the Spirit's work in prophetic inspiration is provided by the details which Ezekiel gives of the Spirit's mode of dealing with him in communicating his visions. While the richness of the prophetic endowment is indicated to us by Micah (3:8): "But I truly am full of power by the Spirit of the Lord, and of judgment, and of might, to declare unto Jacob his transgression, and to Israel his sin." There are, however, two passages that speak quite generally of the whole body of prophets as Spirit-led men, which, in their brief explicitness, deserve to be called the classical passages as to prophetic inspiration. In one of these,— the great psalm-prayer of the Levites recorded in the ninth chapter of Nehemiah,— God is first lauded for "giving His good Spirit to instruct" His people, by the mouth of Moses; and then further praised for enduring this people through so many years and "testifying against them by His Spirit through His prophets" (Neh. 9:20, 30). Here the prophets are conceived as a body of official messengers, through whom the Spirit of God made known His will to His people through all the ages. In exactly similar wise, Zechariah testifies that the Lord of Hosts had sent His words "by His Spirit by the hand of the former prophets" (Zech. 7:12). These are quite comprehensive statements. They include the whole series of the prophets, and they represent them as the official mouthpieces of the Spirit of God, serving the people of God as His organs.[39]

It is sufficiently clear that an official character attaches to all the manifestations of what we have called the theocratic Spirit. The theocratic Spirit appears to be represented as the executive of the Godhead within the sacred nation, the divine power working in the nation for the protection, governing, instruction and leading of the people to its destined goal. The Levitical prayer in the ninth chapter of Nehemiah traces the history of God's people with great fullness; and all through this history represents God as not only looking down from heaven upon His people, leading them, but, as it were, working within them, inspiring organs for their government and instruction,— "clothing Himself with these" organs as the media of His working, as the expressive Hebrew sometimes suggests (Judges 6:34, 1 Chron. 12:18, 2 Chron. 24:20). The aspect in which the theocratic Spirit seems to be conceived is as God in His people, manifesting Himself through inspired instruments in supernatural leading and teaching. Very illuminating as to the mode of His working are the instructions given to Zerubbabel through the prophets Zechariah and Haggai. He— and, with him, all the people of the land— is counseled to be strong and of good courage, "for I am with you, saith the Lord of Hosts, according to the word that I covenanted with you when you came out of Egypt, and my Spirit abideth among you: fear ye not" (Hag. 2:5). "This is the word of the Lord unto Zerubbabel, saying, Not by might, nor by power, but by my Spirit, saith the Lord of Hosts" (Zech. 4:6). The mountains of opposition are to be reduced to a plain; but not by armed force. The symbol of the source of strength is the seven lamps burning brightly by virtue of perennial supplies from the living olives growing by their side; thus, by a hidden, divine supply of deathless life, the Church of God lives and prospers in the world. Not indeed as if God so inhabited Israel, that all that the house of Israel does is of the Lord. "Shall it be said, O house of Israel, Is the Spirit of the Lord straitened?— are these his doings? Do not my words do good to him that walketh uprightly?" (Micah 2:7). The gift of the Spirit is only for good. But there is very clearly brought before us here the face and the mode of God's official inspiration. The theocratic Spirit represents, in a word, the presence of God with His people. And in the Old Testament teaching concerning it, is firmly laid the foundation of the Christian doctrine of God in the Church, leading and guiding it, and supplying it with all needed instruction, powers and graces for its preservation in the world.

We must not omit to observe that in this higher sphere of the theocratic Spirit, the freedom and, so to speak, detachment of the informing Spirit is even more thoroughly guarded than in the case of His cosmical relations. If in the lower sphere the Spirit hovered over rather than was submerged in matter, so here He acts upon His chosen organs in the same sense from without, so that it is impossible to confound His official gifts with their native powers, however exalted. The Spirit here, too, is given by God (Num. 11:29, Isa. 42:1). God puts it on men or fills men with it (Num. 11:25, Ex. 28:3, 31:3); or the Spirit comes (Judg. 3:10, 11:29), comes mightily (14:6, 19, etc., 1 Sam. 11:6) upon men, falls on them (Ezek. 11:5), breaks in upon them, seizes them violently, as it were, and puts them on as a garment (Judg. 6:34). And this is no less true of the prophets than of the other organs of the Spirit's theocratic work: they are all the instruments of a mighty power, which, though in one sense it is conceived as the endowment of the theocratic people, in another sense is conceived as seizing upon its organs from without and above. And "because it is thus fundamentally a power seizing man powerfully, often violently," it is often replaced by the locution, "the hand of Jehovah,"[40] which is, in this usage, the equivalent of the Spirit of Jehovah (2 Kgs. 3:15, Ezek. 1:3, 3:14, 22, 33:22, 37:1, 40:1). The intermittent character of the theocratic gifts still further emphasized their gift by a personal Spirit working purposively. They were not permanent possessions of the theocratic organs, to be used according to their own will, but came and went according to the divine gift.[41] The theocratic gifts of the Spirit are, in a word, everywhere emphatically gifts *from* God as well as *of* God; and every tendency to conceive of them as formally the result of a general inspiration of the nation instead of a special inspiration of the chosen organs is rebuked by every allusion to them. God working in and through man, by whatever variety of inspiration, works divinely and from above. He is no more merged in His church than in the creation, but is, in all His operations alike, the free, transcendent Spirit, dividing to each man severally as He will.

The representations concerning the official theocratic Spirit culminate in Isaiah's prophetic descriptions of the Spirit-endowed Messiah:

> "And there shall come forth a shoot out of the stock of Jesse, and a branch out of his roots shall bear fruit: and the Spirit of the Lord shall rest upon him, the Spirit of wisdom and understanding, the Spirit of counsel and might, the Spirit of knowledge and of the fear of the Lord; and his delight shall be in the fear of the Lord: and he shall not judge after the sight of his eyes, neither reprove after the hearing of his ears: but with righteousness shall he judge the poor, and reprove with equity for the meek of the earth: and he shall smite the earth with the rod of his mouth, and with the breath of his lips shall he slay the wicked. And righteousness shall be the girdle of his loins, and faithfulness the girdle of his reins" (Isa. 11:1 *sq.*).
>
> "Behold my servant whom I uphold; my chosen in whom my soul

delighteth: I have put my Spirit upon him; he shall bring forth judgment to the Gentiles. . . . He shall bring forth judgment in truth. He shall not fail nor be discouraged, till he have set judgment in the earth; and the isles shall wait for his law. Thus saith God the Lord, he that created the heavens, and stretched them forth, he that spread abroad the earth and that which cometh out of it; he that giveth breath unto the people upon it and Spirit to them that walk therein; I the LORD have called thee in righteousness, and will hold thine hand and will keep thee, and give thee for a covenant of the people, for a light of the Gentiles; to open the blind eyes, to bring out the prisoners from the dungeon, and them that sit in darkness out of the prison-house. I am the Lord: that is my name: and my glory will I not give to another, neither my praise unto graven images" (Isa. 42:1 *sq.*).

"The Spirit of the Lord God is upon me"— this is the response of the Messiah to such gracious promises— "because the Lord hath anointed me to preach good tidings unto the meek; he hath sent me to bind up the broken hearted, to proclaim liberty to the captives, and the opening of the prison to them that are bound; to proclaim the acceptable year of the Lord, and the day of vengeance of our God; to comfort all that mourn; to appoint unto them that mourn in Zion, to give unto them a garland for ashes, the oil of gladness for mourning, the garment of praise for the spirit of heaviness; that they might be called trees of righteousness, the planting of the Lord, that he might be glorified" (Isa. 61:1 *sq.*).

No one will fail to observe in these beautiful descriptions of the endowment of the Messiah, how all the theocratic endowments which had been given separately to others unite upon Him; so that all previous organs of the Spirit appear but as partial types of Him to whom as we are told in the New Testament, God "giveth not the Spirit by measure" (John 3:34). Here we perceive the difference between the Messiah and other recipients of the Spirit. To them the Spirit had been "meted out" (Isa. 40:13), according to their place and function in the development of the kingdom of God; upon Him it was poured out without measure, By Him, accordingly, the kingdom of God is consummated. The descriptions of the spiritual endowments of the Messiah are descriptions also, as will no doubt have been noted, of the consummated kingdom of God. His endowment also was not for himself but for the kingdom; it, too, was official. Nevertheless, it was the source in Him of all personal graces also, the opulence and perfection of which are fully described. And thus He becomes the type not only of the theocratic work of the Spirit, but also of His work upon the individual soul, perfecting it after the image of God.

THE INDIVIDUAL SPIRIT

(2) And this brings us naturally to the second aspect in which the Spirit is presented to us in relation to the new creation— His relation to the individual soul, working inwardly in the spirits of men, fitting the children of God for the kingdom of God, even as, working in the nation as such, He, as theocratic Spirit, was preparing God's kingdom for His people. In this aspect He appears specifically as the Spirit of grace. As He is the source of all cosmical life, and of all theocratic life, so is He also the source of all spiritual life, He upholds the soul in being and governs it as part of the great world He has created; He makes it sharer in the theocratic blessings which He brings to His people; but He deals with it, too, within, conforming it to its ideal. In a word, the Spirit of God, in the Old Testament, is not merely the immanent Spirit, the source of all the world's life and all the world's movement; and not merely the inspiring Spirit, the source of His church's strength and safety and of its development in accordance with its special mission; He is as well the indwelling Spirit of holiness in the hearts of God's children. As Hermann Schultz puts it: "The mysterious impulses which enable a man to lead a life well-pleasing to God, are not regarded as a development of human environment, but are nothing else than 'the Spirit of God,' which is also called as being the Spirit peculiarly God's— His Holy Spirit."[42]

We have already had occasion to note that these personal effects of the Spirit's work are sometimes very closely connected with others of His operations. Already as the immanent Spirit of life, indeed, as we saw, there did not lack a connection of His activity with ethical considerations (Gen. 6:3). We will remember, too, that Nehemiah recalls the goodness— i.e., possibly the graciousness— of the Spirit, when He came to instruct Israel in the person of Moses in the wilderness: "Thou gavest also thy good Spirit to instruct them" (Neh. 9:20).[43] When the Spirit came upon Saul, endowing him for his theocratic work, it is represented as having also a very far-reaching personal effect upon him, "The Spirit of the Lord will come mightily upon thee," says Samuel, "and thou shalt prophesy with them, and shalt be turned into another man" (1 Sam. 10:6). "And it was so," adds the narrative, "that when he had turned his back to go from Samuel, God gave him a new heart," or, as the Hebrew has it, "turned him a new heart." Possibly such revolutionary ethical consequences ordinarily attended the official gift of the Spirit, so that the gloss may be a true one which makes 2 Peter 1:21 declare that they were "holy men of God" who spake as they were moved by the Holy Spirit.[44]

At all events this conception of a thorough ethical change characterizes the Old Testament idea of the inner work of the Spirit of Holiness, as He first comes to be called in the Psalms and Isaiah (Ps. 51:11; Isa. 63:10, 11 only).[45] The classical passage in this connection is the Fifty-first Psalm— David's cry of penitence and prayer for mercy after Nathan's probing of his sin with Bathsheba. He prays for the creation within him of a new heart and the renewal of a right spirit within him; and he represents that all his hopes of continued power of new life rest on the continuance of God's holy Spirit, or of the Spirit of God's holiness, with him. Possibly the Spirit is here called holy, primarily, because He is one who cannot dwell in a wicked heart; but it seems also to be implicated that David looks upon Him as the author within him of that holiness without which he cannot hope to see the Lord. A like conception meets us in another Psalm ascribed to David, the One Hundred and Forty-third "Teach me to do thy will; for thou art my God: thy Spirit is good; lead me in the land of uprightness." The two conceptions of the divine grace and holiness are also combined by Isaiah in an account of how Israel had been, since the days of Moses, dealing ungratefully with God, and, by their rebellion, grieving "the Holy Spirit whom He had graciously put in the midst of them" (Isa. 63:10, 11).[46] The conception may primarily be that the Spirit given to guide Israel was a Spirit of holiness in the sense that He could not brook sin in those with whom He dealt, but the conception that He would guide them in ways of holiness underlies that.

This aspect of the work of the Spirit of God is most richly developed, however, in prophecies of the future. In the Messianic times, Isaiah tells us, the Spirit shall be poured out from on high with the effect that judgment shall dwell in the wilderness and righteousness shall abide in the peaceful field (Isa. 32:15). It is in such descriptions of the Messianic era as a time of the reign of the Spirit in the hearts of the people, that the opulence of His saving influences is developed. It is He who shall gather the children of God into the kingdom, so that no one shall be missing (Isa. 34:16). It is He who, as the source of all blessings, shall be poured out on the seed with the result that it shall spring up in the luxuriant growth and bear such rich fruitage that one shall cry 'I am the Lord's,' and another shall call himself by the name of Jacob, and another shall write on his hand, 'Unto the Lord,' and shall surname himself by the name of Israel (Isa. 44:3 sq.). It is His abiding presence which constitutes the preeminent blessing of the new covenant which Jehovah makes with His people in the day of redemption: "And as for me, this is my covenant with them, saith the Lord: my Spirit that is upon thee, and my words which I have put in thy mouth, shall not depart out of thy mouth, nor out of the mouth of thy seed, nor out of the mouth of thy seed's seed, saith the Lord, from henceforth and forever" (Isa. 59:21). The gift of the Spirit as an abiding presence in the heart of the individual is the crowning Messianic blessing. To precisely the same effect is the teaching of Ezekiel. The new heart and new spirit is one of the burdens of his message (11:19, 18:31, 36:26): and these are the Messianic gifts of God to His people through the Spirit. God's people are dead; but He will open their graves and cause them to come up out of their graves: "And I will put my Spirit in you, and ye shall live" (37:14). They are in captivity; he will bring them out of captivity: "Neither will I hide my face any more from them: for I have poured out my Spirit upon the house of Israel, saith the Lord God" (39:29). Like promises appear in Zechariah: "And I will pour upon the house of David, and upon the inhabitants of Jerusalem, the Spirit of grace and supplication; and they shall look upon me whom they have pierced" (12:10). It is the converting Spirit of God that is spoken of. One thing only is left to complete the picture— the clear declaration that, in these coming days of blessing, the Spirit hitherto given only to Israel shall be poured out upon the whole world. This Joel gives us in that wonderful passage which is applied by Peter to the outpouring begun at Pentecost: "And it shall come to pass afterward," says the Lord God through His prophet, "that I will pour out my Spirit upon all flesh:. . . and also upon the servants and upon the handmaids in those days will I pour out my Spirit. . . . And it shall come to pass, that whosoever shall call on the name of the Lord shall be delivered" (2:28-32).

In this series of passages, the indwelling Spirit of the New Testament is obviously brought before us— the indwelling God, author of all holiness and of all salvation. Thus there are firmly laid by them the foundations of the Christian doctrine of Regeneration and Sanctification,— of God in the soul quickening its powers of spiritual life and developing it in holiness. Nor can it be a ground of wonder that this aspect of His work is less frequently dwelt upon than His theocratic activities; nor that it is chiefly in prophecies of the future that the richer references to it occur.[47] This was the time of theocratic development; the old dispensation was a time of preparation for the fullness of spiritual graces. It is rather a ground of wonder that even in few and scattered hints and in prophecies of the times of the Spirit yet to come, such a deep and thorough grasp upon His individual work should be exhibited.

By its presentation of this work of the Spirit in the heart, the Old Testament completes its conception of the Spirit of God— the great conception of the immanent, inspiring, indwelling God. In it the three great ideas are thrown prominently forward, of God in the world, God in the Church, God in the soul: the God of Providence, the immanent source of all that comes to pass, the director and governor of the world of matter and spirit alike; the God of the Church, the inspiring source of all Church life and of all Church gifts, through which the Church is instructed, governed, preserved and extended; and the God of grace, the indwelling source of all holiness and of all religious aspirations, emotions and activities. Attention has already been called to the great enrichment which was brought to the general conception of God by this doctrine of the Spirit of God in its first aspect. The additional aspects in which He is presented in the pages of the Old Testament of course still further enrich and elevate the conception. By throwing a still stronger emphasis on the personality of the Spirit they made even wider the great gulf that already yawned between all Pantheising notions and the Biblical doctrine of the Personal God, the immanent source of all that comes to pass. And they bring out with great force and clearness the conceptions of grace and holiness as inherent in the idea of God working, and thus operate to deepen the ethical conception of the divine Being. It is only as a personal, choosing, gracious and holy God, who bears His people on His heart for good, and who seeks to conform them in life and character to His own holiness— that we can conceive the God of the Old Testament, if we will attend to its doctrine of the Spirit. Thus the fundamental unity of the conception with that of the Holy Spirit of the New Testament grows ever more obvious, the more attentively it is considered. The Spirit of God of the Old Testament performs all the functions which are ascribed to the Holy Spirit of the New Testament, and bears all the same characteristics. They are conceived alike both in their nature and in their operations. We cannot help identifying them.

Such an identification need not involve, however, the assertion that the Spirit of God was conceived in the Old Testament as the Holy Spirit is in the New, as a distinct hypostasis in the divine nature. Whether this be so, or, if so in some measure, how far it may be true, is a matter for separate investigation. The Spirit of God certainly acts as a person and is presented to us as a person, throughout the Old Testament. In no passage is He conceived otherwise than personally— as a free, willing, intelligent being. This is, however, in itself only the pervasive testimony of the Scriptures to the personality of God. For it is equally true that the Spirit of God is everywhere in the Old Testament identified with God. This is only its pervasive testimony to the divine unity. The question for examination is, how far the one personal God was conceived of as embracing in His unity hypostatical distinctions. This question is a very complicated one and needs very delicate treatment. There are, indeed, three questions included in the general one, which for the sake of clearness we ought to keep apart. We may ask, May the Christian properly see in the Spirit of God of the Old Testament the personal Holy Spirit of the New? This we may answer at once in the affirmative. We may ask again, Are there any hints in the Old Testament anticipating and adumbrating the revelation of the hypostatic Spirit of the New? This also, it seems, we ought to answer in the affirmative. We may ask again, Are these hints of such clearness as actually to reveal this doctrine, apart from the revelation of the New Testament? This should be doubtless answered in the negative. There are hints, and they serve for points of attachment for the fuller New Testament teaching. But they are only hints, and, apart from the New Testament teaching, would be readily explained as personifications or ideal objectivations of the power of God. Undoubtedly, side by side with the stress put upon the unity of God and the identity of the Spirit with the God who gives it, there is a distinction recognized between God and His

Spirit— in the sense at least of a discrimination between God over all and God in all, between the Giver and the Given, between the Source and the Executor of the moral law. This distinction already emerges in Genesis 1:2; and it does not grow less observable as we advance through the Old Testament. It is prominent in the standing phrases by which, on the one hand, God is spoken of as sending, putting, placing, pouring, emptying His Spirit upon man, and on the other the Spirit is spoken of as coming, resting, falling, springing upon man. There is a sort of objectifying of the Spirit over against God in both cases; in the former case, by sending Him from Himself God, as it were, separates Him from Himself; in the latter, He appears almost as a distinct person, acting *sua sponte*. Schultz does not hesitate to speak of the Spirit even in Genesis 1:2 as appearing "as very independent, just like a hypostasis or person."[48] Kleinert finds in this passage at least a tendency toward hypostatizing— though he thinks this tendency was not subsequently worked out.[49] Perhaps we are warranted in saying as much as this— that there is observable in the Old Testament, not, indeed, an hypostatizing of the Spirit of God, but a tendency toward it— that, in Hofmann's cautious language, the Spirit appears in the Old Testament "as somewhat distinct from the 'I' of God which God makes the principle of life in the world.[50] A preparation, at least, for the full revelation of the Trinity in the New Testament is observable;[51] points of connection with it are discoverable; and so Christians are able to read the Old Testament without offense, and to find without confusion their own Holy Spirit in its Spirit of God.[52]

More than this could scarcely be looked for. The elements in the doctrine of God which above all others needed emphasis in Old Testament times were naturally His unity and His personality. The great thing to be taught the ancient people of God was that the God of all the earth is one person. Over against the varying idolatries about them, this was the truth of truths of which Israel was primarily to stand; and not until this great truth was ineffaceably stamped upon their souls could the personal distinctions in the Triune-God be safely made known to them. A premature revelation of the Spirit as a distinct hypostasis could have wrought nothing but harm to the people of God. We shall all no doubt agree with Kleinert[53] that it is pragmatic in Isidore of Pelusium to say that Moses knew the doctrine of the Trinity well enough, but concealed it through fear that Polytheism would profit by it. But we may safely affirm this of God the Revealer, in the gradual delivery of the truth concerning Himself to men. He reveals the whole truth, but in divers portions and in divers manners: and it was incident to the progressive delivery of doctrine that the unity of the Godhead should first be made the firm possession of men, and the Trinity in that unity should be unveiled to them only afterwards, when the times were ripe for it. What we need wonder over is not that the hypostatical distinctness of the Spirit is not more clearly revealed in the Old Testament but that the approaches to it are laid so skillfully that the doctrine of the hypostatical Holy Spirit of the New Testament finds so many and such striking points of attachment in the Old Testament, and yet no Israelite had ever been disturbed in repeating with hearty faith his great Shema, "Hear O Israel, the Lord our God is one Lord" (Deut. 6:4). Not until the whole doctrine of the Trinity was ready to be manifested in such visible form as at the baptism of Christ— God in heaven, God on earth and God descending from heaven to earth— could any part of the mystery be safely uncovered.

There yet remains an important query which we cannot pass wholly by. We have seen the rich development of the doctrine of the Spirit in the Old Testament. We have seen the testimony the Old Testament bears to the activity of the Spirit of God throughout the old dispensation. What then is meant by calling the new dispensation the dispensation of the Spirit? What does John (7:39) mean by saying that the Spirit was not yet given because Jesus was not yet glorified? What our Lord Himself, when He promised the Comforter, by saying that the Comforter would not come until He went away and sent Him (John 16:7); and by breathing on His disciples, saying, "Receive ye the Holy Spirit" (John 20:22)? What did the descent of the Spirit at Pentecost mean, when He came to inaugurate the dispensation of the Spirit? It cannot be meant that the Spirit was not active in the old dispensation. We have already seen that the New Testament writers themselves represent Him to have been active in the old dispensation in all the varieties of activity with which He is active in the new. Such passages seem to have diverse references. Some of them may refer to the specifically miraculous endowments which characterized the apostles and the churches which they founded.[54] Others refer to the worldwide mission of the Spirit, promised, indeed, in the Old Testament, but only now to be realized. But there is a more fundamental idea to be reckoned with still. This is the idea of the preparatory nature of the Old Testament dispensation. The old dispensation was a preparatory one and must be strictly conceived as such. What spiritual blessings came to it were by way of prelibation.[55] They were many and various. The Spirit worked in Providence no less universally then than now. All the good that was in the world was then as now due to Him. All the hope of God's Church then as now depended on Him. Every grace of the godly life then as now was a fruit of His working. But the object of the whole dispensation was only to prepare for the outpouring of the Spirit upon all flesh. He kept the remnant safe and pure; but it was primarily only in order that the seed might be preserved. This was the fundamental end of His activity, then. The dispensation of the Spirit, properly so-called, did not dawn until the period of preparation was over and the day of outpouring had come. The mustard seed had been preserved through all the ages only by the Spirit's brooding care. Now it is planted, and it is by His operation that it is growing up into a great tree which shades the whole earth, and to the branches of which all the fowls of heaven come for shelter. It is not that His work is more real in the new dispensation than in the old. It is not merely that it is more universal. It is that it is directed to a different end— that it is no longer for the mere preserving of the seed unto the day of planting, but for the perfecting of the fruitage and the gathering of the harvest. The Church, to use a figure of Isaiah's, was then like a pent-in stream; it is now like that pent-in stream with the barriers broken down and the Spirit of the Lord driving it (Cf. Isa. 59:19). It was He who preserved it in being when it was pent-in. It is He who is now driving on its gathered floods till it shall cover the earth as the waters cover the sea. In one word, that was a day in which the Spirit restrained His power. Now the great day of the Spirit is come!

15

On the Doctrine of the Holy Spirit

An Introduction to *The Work of the Holy Spirit* by Abraham Kuyper

It is fortunately no longer necessary formally to introduce Dr. Kuyper to the American religious public. Quite a number of his remarkable essays have appeared of late years in our periodicals. These have borne such titles as "Calvinism in Art," "Calvinism the Source and Pledge of Our Constitutional Liberties," "Calvinism and Confessional Revision," "The Obliteration of Boundaries," "The Antithesis Between Symbolism and Revelation"; and have appeared in the pages of such publications as *Christian Thought, Bibliotheca Sacra, The Presbyterian and Reformed Review*— not, we may be sure, without delighting their readers with the breadth of their treatment and the high and penetrating quality of their thought. The columns of *The Christian Intelligencer* have from time to time during the last year been adorned with examples of Dr. Kuyper's practical expositions of Scriptural truth; and now and again a brief but illuminating discussion of a topic of present interest has appeared in the columns of *The Independent.* The appetite whetted by this taste of good things has been partially gratified by the publication in English of two extended treatises from his hand— one discussing in a singularly profound way the principles of *The Encyclopedia of Sacred Theology* (Charles Scribner's Sons, 1898), and the other expounding with the utmost breadth and forcefulness the fundamental principles of *Calvinism* (The Fleming H. Revell Company, 1899). The latter volume consists of lectures delivered on "The L. P. Stone Foundation" at Princeton Theological Seminary in the autumn of 1898, and Dr. Kuyper's visit to America on this occasion brought him into contact with many lovers of high ideas in America, and has left a sense of personal acquaintance with him on the minds of multitudes who had the good fortune to meet him or hear his voice at that time. It is impossible for us to look longer upon Dr. Kuyper as a stranger, needing an introduction to our favorable notice, when he appears again before us; he seems rather now to be one of our own prophets to whose message we have a certain right, and a new book from whose hands we welcome as we would a new gift from our dear friend charged in a sense with care for our welfare. The book that is at present offered to the American public does not indeed come fresh from his hands. It has already been within the reach of his Dutch audience for more than a decade (it was published in 1888). It is only recently, however, that Dr. Kuyper has come to belong to us also, and the publication of this book in English, we may hope, is only another step in the process which will gradually make all his message ours.

Certainly no one will turn over the pages of this volume— much less will he, as our Jewish friends would say, "sink himself into the book"— without perceiving that it is a very valuable gift which comes to us from our newly found teacher. It is, as will be at once observed, a comprehensive treatise on the Work of the Holy Spirit— a theme higher than which none can occupy the attention of the Christian man, and yet one on which really comprehensive treatises are comparatively rare. It is easy, to be sure, to exaggerate the significance of the latter fact. There never was a time, of course, when Christians did not confess their faith in the Holy Spirit; and there never was a time when they did not speak to one another of the work of the Blessed Spirit, the Executor of the Godhead not only in creation and upholding of the worlds and in the inspiration of the prophets and apostles, but also in the regenerating and sanctifying of the soul. Nor has there ever been a time when, in the prosecution of its task of realizing mentally the treasures of truth put in its charge in the Scriptural revelation, the Church has not busied itself also with the investigation of the mysteries of the person and work of the Spirit; and especially has there never been a time since that tremendous revival of religion which we call the Reformation when the whole work of the Spirit in the application of the redemption wrought out by Christ has not been a topic of the most thorough and loving study of Christian men. Indeed, it partly arises out of the very intensity of the study given to the saving activities of the Spirit that so few comprehensive treatises on the work of the Spirit have been written. The subject has seemed so vast, the ramifications of it have appeared so far-reaching, that few have had the courage to undertake it as a whole. Dogmaticians have, to be sure, been compelled to present the entire range of the matter in its appropriate place in their completed systems. But when monographs came to be written, they have tended to confine themselves to a single segment of the great circle; and thus we have had treatises rather on, say, Regeneration, or Justification, or Sanctification, on the Anointing of the Spirit, or the Intercession of the Spirit, or the sealing of the Spirit, than on the work of the Spirit as a whole. It would be a great mistake to think of the doctrine of the Holy Spirit as neglected, merely because it has been preferably presented under its several rubrics or parts, rather than in its entirety. How easily one may fall into such an error is fairly illustrated by certain criticisms that have been recently passed upon the Westminster Confession of Faith— which is (as a Puritan document was sure to be) very much a treatise on the work of the Spirit— as if it were deficient, in not having a chapter specially devoted to "the Holy Spirit and His Work."[56] The sole reason why it does not give *a* chapter to this subject, however, is because it prefers to give *nine* chapters to it; and when an attempt was made to supply the fancied omission, it was found that pretty much all that could be done was to present in the proposed new chapter a meager summary of the contents of these nine chapters. It would have been more plausible, indeed, to say that the Westminster confession comparatively neglected the work of Christ, or even the work of God the Father. Similarly the lack in our literature of a large number of comprehensive treatises on the work of the Holy Spirit is in part due to the richness of our literature in treatises on the separate portions of that work severally. The significance of Dr. Kuyper's book is, therefore, in part due only to the fact that he has had the courage to attack and the gifts successfully to accomplish a task which few have possessed the breadth either of outlook or of powers to undertake. And it is no small gain to be able to survey the whole field of the work of the Holy Spirit in its organic unity under the guidance of so fertile, so systematic, and so practical a mind. If we cannot look upon it as breaking entirely new ground, or even say that it is the only work of its kind since John Owen, we can at least say that it brings together the material belonging to this great topic with a systematizing genius that is very rare, and presents it with a penetrating appreciation of its meaning and a richness of apprehension of its relations that is exceedingly illuminating.

It is to be observed that we have not said without qualification that the comparative rarity of such comprehensive treatises on the work of the Holy Spirit as Dr. Kuyper's is due simply to the greatness and difficulty of the task. We have been careful to say that it is only in part due to this cause. It is only in the circles to which this English translation is presented, to say the truth, that this remark is applicable at all. It is the happiness of the Reformed Christians of English speech that they are the heirs of what must in all fairness be spoken of as an immense literature upon this great topic; it may even be said with some justice that the peculiarity of their theological labor turns just on the diligence and depth of their study of this *locus*. It is, it will be remembered, to John Owen's great *Discourse Concerning the Holy Spirit* that Dr. Kuyper points as hitherto the normative treatise on the subject. But John Owen's book did not stand alone in his day and generation, but was rather merely symptomatic of the engrossment of the theological thought of the circle of which he was so great an ornament in the investigation of this subject. Thomas Goodwin's treatise on *The Work of the Holy Ghost in Our Salvation* is well worthy of a place by its side; and it is only the truth to say that Puritan thought was almost entirely occupied with loving study of the work of the Holy Spirit, and found its highest expression in dogmatico-practical expositions of the several aspects of it— of which such treatises as those of Charnock and Swinnerton on Regeneration are only the best-known examples among a multitude which have fallen out of memory in the lapse of years. For a century and a half afterward, indeed, this topic continued to form the hinge of the theologizing of the English Nonconformists. Nor has it lost its central position even yet in the minds of those who have the best right to be looked upon as the successors of the Puritans. There has been in some quarters some decay, to be sure, in sureness of grasp and theological precision in the presentation of the subject; but it is possible that a larger number of practical treatises on some element or other of the doctrine of the Spirit continue to appear from the English press annually than on any other branch of divinity. Among these, such books as Dr. A. J. Gordon's *The Ministry of the Spirit,* Dr. E. J. Cumming's *Through the Eternal Spirit,* Principal H. C. G. Moule's *Veni Creator,* Dr. R. A. Redford's *Vox Dei,* Dr. J. Robson's *The Holy Spirit, the Paraclete,* Dr. C. R. Vaughan's *The Gifts of the Holy Spirit* [57]— to name only a few of the most recent books— attain a high level of theological clarity and spiritual power; while, if we may be permitted to go back only a few years, we may find in Dr. James Buchanan's *The Office and Work of he Holy Spirit,* and in Dr. George Smeaton's *The Doctrine of the Holy Spirit,* two treatises covering the whole ground — the one in a more practical, the other in a more didactic spirit— in a manner worthy of the best tradition of our Puritan fathers.[58] There has always been a copious stream of literature on the work of the Holy Spirit, therefore, among the English-speaking churches; and Dr. Kuyper's book comes to us not as something of a novelty, but as a specially finely conceived and executed presentation of a topic on which we are all thinking.

But the case is not the same in all parts of Christendom. If we lift our eyes from our own special condition and view the Church at large, it is a very different spectacle that greets them. As we sweep them down the history of the Church, we discover that the topic of the work of the Holy Spirit was one which only at a late date really emerged as the explicit study of Christian men. As we sweep them over the whole extent of the modern Church, we discover that it is a topic which appeals even yet with little force to very large sections of the Church. The poverty of Continental theology in this *locus* is, indeed, after all is said and done, depressing. Note one or two little French books, by E. Guers and G. Tophel, and a couple of formal studies of the New Testament doctrine of the Spirit by the Dutch writers Stemler and Thoden Van Velzen, called out by The Hague Society— and we have before us almost the whole list of the older books of our century which pretend in any way to cover the ground.[59] Nor has very much been done more recently to remedy the deficiency. The amazing theological activity of latter-day Germany has, to be sure, not been able to pass so fruitful a theme entirely by; and her scholars have given us a few scientific studies of sections of the Biblical material... In fact, only in a single instance in the whole history of German theological literature— or, we may say, prior to Dr. Kuyper in the entire history of Continental theological literature— has anyone had the courage or found the impulse to face the task Dr. Kuyper has so admirably executed. We are referring, of course, to the great work on *Die Lehre vom heiligen Geiste,*[60] which was projected by that theological giant, K.A. Kahnis, but the first part of which only was published— in a thin volume of three hundred and fifty-six pages, in 1847. It was doubtless symptomatic of the state of feeling in Germany on the subject that Kahnis never found time or encouragement in a long life of theological pursuits to complete his book. And, indeed, it was greeted in theological circles at the time with something like amused amazement that anyone could devote so much time and labor to this theme, or expect others to find time and energy to read such a treatise. We are told that a well-known theologian remarked caustically of it that if things were to be carried out on that scale, no one could expect to live long enough to read the literature of his subject; and the similar remark made by C. Hase in the preface to the fifth edition of his *Dogmatik,* though it names no names, is said to have had Kahnis's book in view.[61] The significance of Kahnis's unique and unsuccessful attempt to provide for German Protestantism some worthy treatment of the doctrine of the Holy Spirit is so great that it will repay us to fix the facts concerning it well in our minds. And to this end we extract the following account of it from the introduction of the work of von Lechler entitled *Die biblische Lehre vom heiligen Geiste*[62] (1899):

> "We have to indicate, in conclusion, another circumstance in the history of our doctrine, which is in its way just as significant for the attitude of present-day science toward this topic as was the silence of the first Ecumenical Council concerning it for the end of the first theological age. It is the extraordinary poverty of the monographs on the Holy Spirit. Although there do exist some, and in some instances important, studies dealing with the subject, yet their number is out of all proportion to the greatness and extent of the problems. We doubtless should not err in assuming that vital interest in a scientific question will express itself not merely in comprehensive handbooks and encyclopedic compendiums, the latter of which are especially forced to see the completeness of the list of subjects treated, but of necessity also in those separate investigations in which especially the fresh vigor of youth is accustomed to make proof of its fitness for higher studies. What *lacunae* we should have to regret in other

branches of theological science if a rich development of monographic literature did not range itself by the side of the compendiums, breaking out here and
there new paths, laying deeper foundations, supplying valuable material for the
constructive or decorative completion of the scientific structure! All this, in the
present instance, however, has scarcely made a beginning. The sole separate
treatise which has been projected on a really profound and broad basis of investigation— the *Lehre vom heiligen Geiste* of K. A. Kahnis (then at Breslau),
1847 — came to a standstill with its first part. This celebrated theologian, who
had certainly in his possession in surprising measure the qualities and acquisi-
tions that fitted him to come forward as a preparer of the way in this uncertain
and little worthily studied subject, had set before himself the purpose of inves-
tigating this, as he himself called it, "extraordinarily neglected" topic, at once
on its Biblical, ecclesiastical, historical, and dogmatic sides. The history of his
book is exceedingly instructive and suggestive with respect to the topic itself.
He found the subject, as he approached it more closely, in a very special degree
a difficult one, chiefly on account of the manifoldness of the conception. At
first his results became ever more and more negative. A controversy with the
"friends of light"[63] of the time helped him forward. *Testium nubes magis juvant,
quam luciferorum virorum importuna lumina.*[64] But God, he says, led him to
greater clearness: the doctrine of the Church approved itself to him. Nevertheless it was not his purpose to establish the Scriptural doctrine in all its points,
but only to exhibit the place which the Holy Spirit occupies in the development
of the Word of God in the Old and New Testaments. There was a feeling that
came to him that we were standing upon the eve of a new outpouring of the
Spirit. But the wished-for dawn, he says, still held back. . . . His wide survey,
beyond his special subject, of the whole domain of science in the corporate life
of the Church, is characteristic no less of the subject than of the man. It was not
given to him, however, to see the longed-for flood poured over the parched
fields. His exegetical "foundation" (chaps. i-iii) moves in the old tracks. Since
he shared essentially the subjective point of view of Schleiermacher[65] and committed the final decision in the determining conceptions to philosophy, in spite
of many remarkable flashes of insight into the Scriptures he remained fixed in
the intellectualistic and ethical mode of conceiving the Holy Spirit, though this
was accompanied by many attempts to transcend Schleiermacher, but without
attaining of any unitary conception and without any effort to bring to a Scriptural solution the burning question of the personality or impersonality of the
Spirit. The fourth chapter institutes a comparison between the Spirit of Christianity and that of heathenism. The second book deals first with the relation of
the Church to the Holy Spirit in general, and then enters upon a history of the
doctrine, which is carried, however, only through the earliest Fathers, and breaks
off with a survey of the scanty harvest which the first age supplied to the suc-
ceeding epochs, in which the richest development of the doctrine took place.
Here the book closes. . . ."[66]

Thus the only worthy attempt German theology has made to produce a comprehensive treatise on the work of the Holy Spirit remains a neglected *torso* till today.

The Holy Spirit

If we will gather up the facts to which we have thus somewhat desultorily called attention into a propositional statement, we shall find ourselves compelled to recognize that the doctrine of the Holy Spirit was only slowly brought to the explicit consciousness of the Church, and has even yet taken a firm hold on the mind and consciousness of only a small section of the Church. To be more specific, we shall need to note that the early Church busied itself with the investigation within the limits of this *locus* of only the doctrine of the person of the Holy Spirit— His deity and personality— and of His one function of inspirer of the prophets and apostles, while the whole doctrine of the work of the Spirit at large is a gift to the Church from the Reformation;[67] and we shall need to note further that since its formulation by the Reformers this doctrine has taken deep root and borne its full fruits only in the Reformed churches, and among them in exact proportion to the loyalty of their adherence to, and the richness of their development of, the fundamental principles of the Reformed theology. Stated in its sharpest form this is as much as to say that the developed doctrine of the work of the Holy Spirit is an exclusively Reformation doctrine, and more particularly a Reformed doctrine, and more particularly still a Puritan doctrine. Wherever the fundamental principles of the Reformation have gone, it has gone; but it has come to its full rights only among Reformed churches, and among them only where what we have been accustomed to call "the Second Reformation"[68] has deepened the spiritual life of the churches and cast back the Christian with special poignancy of feeling upon the grace of God alone as his sole dependence for salvation and all the goods of this life and the life to come. Indeed, it is possible to be more precise still. The doctrine of the work of the Holy Spirit is a gift from John Calvin to the Church of Christ. He did not, of course, invent it. The whole of it lay spread out on the pages of Scripture with a clearness and fullness of utterance which one would think would secure that even he who ran should read it; and doubtless he who ran did read it, and it has fed the soul of the true believer in all ages. Accordingly, hints of its apprehension are found widely scattered in all Christian literature, and in particular the germs of the doctrine are spread broadcast over the pages of Augustine. Luther did not fail to lay hold of them; Zwingli shows time and again that he had them richly in his mind; they constituted, in very fact, one of the foundations of the Reformation movement, or rather they provided its vital breath. But it was Calvin who first gave them anything like systematic or adequate expression; and it is through him and from him that they have come to be the assured possession of the Church of Christ.

There is no phenomenon in doctrinal history more astonishing than the commonly entertained views as to the contribution made by John Calvin to the development of Christian doctrine. He is thought of currently as the father of doctrines, such as that of predestination and reprobation, of which he was the mere heir— taking them as wholes over from the hands of his great master Augustine. Meanwhile his real personal contributions to Christian doctrine are utterly forgotten. These are of the richest kind and cannot be enumerated here. But it is germane to our present topic to note that at their head stand three gifts of the first value to the Church's thought and life, which we should by no means allow to pass from our grateful memory. It is to John Calvin that we owe that broad conception of the work of Christ which is expressed in the doctrine of his threefold office of Prophet, Priest, and King. He was the first one who presented the work of Christ under this *schema*[69] and from him it was that it has passed into a Christian commonplace. It is to John Calvin that we owe the whole conception of a science of "Christian Ethics"; for he was the first to outline its idea and develop its principles and contents, and it remained a *peculium*[70] of his followers for a century. And it is to John Calvin that we owe the first formulation of the doctrine of the work of the Holy Spirit. He himself gave it a very rich statement, developing it especially in the broad departments of "Common Grace," "Regeneration," and "the Witness of the Spirit"; and it is, as we have seen, among his spiritual descendants only that it has to this day received any adequate attention in the churches. We must guard ourselves, of course, from exaggeration in such a matter; the bare facts, when put forth without pausing to allow for the unimportant shadings, sound of themselves sufficiently like an exaggeration.[71] But it is simply true that these great topics received their first formulation at the hands of John Calvin; and it is from him that the Church has derived them, and to him that it owes its thanks for them.

And if we pause to ask why the formulation of the doctrine of the work of the Spirit waited for the Reformation and for Calvin, and why the further working out of the details of this doctrine and its enrichment by the profound study of Christian minds and meditation of Christian hearts has come down from Calvin only to the Puritans, and from the Puritans to their spiritual descendants like the Free Church teachers of the Disruption era[72] and the Dutch contestants for the treasures of the Reformed religion of our own day, the reasons are not far to seek. There is, in the first place, a regular order in the acquisition, inherent in the nature of the case, which therefore the Church was bound to follow in its gradual realization of the deposit of truth given it in the Scriptures; and by virtue of this the Church could not successfully attack the task of assimilating and formulating the doctrine of the work of the Spirit until the foundations had been laid firmly in a clear grasp on yet more fundamental doctrines. And there are, in the next place, certain forms of doctrinal construction which leave no or only a meager place for the work of the personal Holy Spirit in the heart; and in the presence of these constructions this doctrine, even where in part apprehended and acknowledged, languishes and falls out of the interest of men. The operation of the former cause postponed the development of the doctrine of the work of the Spirit until the way was prepared for it; and this preparation was complete only at the Reformation. The operation of the second cause has retarded where it has not stifled the proper assimilation of the doctrine in many parts of the Church until today.

To be more specific. The development of the doctrinal system of Christianity in the apprehension of the Church has actually run through— as it theoretically should have run through— a regular and logical course. First, attention was absorbed in the contemplation of the objective elements of the Christian deposit, and only afterward were the subjective elements taken into fuller consideration. First of all it was the Christian doctrine of God that forced itself on the attention of men, and it was not until the doctrine of the Trinity had been thoroughly assimilated that attention was vigorously attracted to the Christian doctrine of the God-man; and again, it was not until the doctrine of the Person of Christ was thoroughly assimilated that attention was poignantly attracted to the Christian doctrine of sin— man's need and helplessness; and only after that had been wrought out fully, again, could attention turn to the objective provision to meet man's needs in the work of Christ; and again, only after that to the subjective provision to meet his needs in the work of the Spirit. This is the logical order of development, and it is the actual order in which the Church has slowly and amid the throes of all sorts of conflicts— with the world and with its own slowness to believe all that the prophets have written— worked its way into the whole truth revealed to it in the Word. The order is, it will be observed, Theology, Christology, Anthropology (Harmartiology), Impetration of Redemption, Application of Redemption[73]; and in the nature of the case the topics that fall under the rubric of the application of redemption could not be solidly investigated until the basis had been laid for them in the assimilation of the preceding topics. We have connected the great names of Athanasius[74] and his worthy successors who fought out the Christological disputes, of Augustine and of Anselm[75], with the precedent stages of this development. It was the leaders of the Reformation who were called on to add the capstone to the structure by working out the facts as to the application of redemption to the soul of man through the Holy Spirit. Some elements of the doctrine of the Spirit are indeed implicated in earlier discussions. For example, the deity and personality of the Spirit— the whole doctrine of his person— was a part of the doctrine of the Trinity, and this accordingly became a topic for early debate, and patristic literature[76] is rich in discussions of it. The authority of Scripture was fundamental to the whole doctrinal discussion, and the doctrine of the inspiration of the prophets and apostles by the Spirit was therefore asserted from the beginning with great emphasis. In the determination of man's need in the Pelagian[77] controversy much was necessarily determined about "Grace"— its necessity, its prevenience, its efficacy, its indefectibility[78]— and in this much was anticipated of what was afterward to be more orderly developed in the doctrine of the interior work of the Spirit; and accordingly there is much in Augustine which preadumbrates the determination of later times. But even in Augustine there is a vagueness and tentativeness in the treatment of these topics which advises us that while the facts relatively to man and his needs and the methods of God's working upon him to salvation are firmly grasped, these same facts relatively to the personal activities of the Spirit as yet await their full assimilation. Another step had yet to be taken: the Church needed to wait yet for Anselm to set on foot the final determination of the doctrine of a vicarious atonement[79]; and only when time had been given for its assimilation, at length men's minds were able to take the final step. Then Luther rose to proclaim justification by faith, and Calvin to set forth with his marvelous balance the whole doctrine of the work of the Spirit in applying salvation to the soul. In this matter, too, the fullness of the times needed to be waited for; and when the fullness of the times came the men were ready for their task and the Church was ready for their work. And in this collection we find a portion of the secret of the immense upheaval of the Reformation.

Unfortunately, however, the Church was not ready in all its parts alike for the new step in doctrinal development. This was, of course, in the nature of the case: for the development of doctrine takes place naturally in a matrix of old and hardened partial conceptions, and can make its way only by means of a conflict of opinion. All Arians did not disappear immediately after the Council of Nicea[80]; on the contrary, for an age they seemed destined to rule the Church. The decree of Chalcedon[81] did not at once quiet all Christological debate, or do away with all Christological error. There were remainders of Pelagianism that outlived Augustine; and indeed that after the Synod of Orange[82] began to make headway against the truth. Anselm's construction of the atonement only slowly worked its way into the hearts of men. And so, when Calvin had for the first time formulated the fuller and more precise doctrine of the work of the Spirit, there were antagonistic forces in the world which crowded upon it and curtailed its influence and clogged its advance in the apprehension of men. In general, these may be said to be two: the sacerdotal tendency on the one hand and the libertarian tendency[83] on the other. The sacerdotal tendency was entrenched in the old Church; from which the Reformers were extruded indeed by the very force of the new leaven of their individualism of spiritual life. That Church was therefore impervious to the newly formulated doctrine of the work of the Spirit. To it the Church was the depository of grace, the sacraments were its indispensable vehicle, and the administration of it lay in the hands of human agents. Wherever this sacramentarianism[84] went, in however small a measure, it tended so far to distract men's attention from the Spirit of God and to focus it on the *media*[85] of His working; and wherever it has entrenched itself, there the study of the work of the Spirit has accordingly more or less languished. It is easy indeed to say that the Spirit stands behind the sacraments and is operative in the sacraments; as a matter of fact, the sacraments tend, in all such cases, to absorb the attention, and the theoretical explanations of their efficacy as vested in the Spirit's energy tend to pass out of the vivid interest of men. The libertarian tendency, on the other hand, was the nerve of the old Semi-Pelagianism[86] which in Thomism[87] and Tridentinism[88] became in a modified form the formal doctrine of the Church of Rome; and in various forms it soon began to step also into and to trouble the churches of the Reformation— first the Lutheran and after that also the Reformed. To it, the will of man was in greater or less measure the decisive factor in the subjective reception of salvation; and in proportion as it was more or less developed or more or less fully applied, interest in the doctrine of the subjective work of the Spirit languished, and in these circles too men's minds were to that degree distracted from the study of the doctrine of the work of the Spirit, and tended to focus themselves on the autocracy of the human will and its native or renewed ability to obey God and seek and find communion with Him. No doubt here too it is easy to point to the function which is still allowed the Spirit, in most at least of the theological constructions on this basis. But the practical effect has been that just in proportion as the autocracy of the human will has been emphasized, the interest in the internal work of the Spirit has declined. When we take into consideration the widespread influence that has been attained even in the Protestant world by these two antagonistic tendencies, we shall cease to wonder at the widespread neglect that has befallen the doctrine of the work of the Spirit. And we shall have prosecuted our inquiry but a little way before we become aware how entirely these facts account for the phenomena before us: how completely it is true that interest in the doctrine of the work of the Spirit has failed just in those regions and just in those epochs in which either sacramentarian or libertarian opinions have ruled; and how true it is that engagement with this doctrine has been intense only along the banks of that narrow stream of religious life and thought the keynote of which has been the *soli Deo gloria*[89] in all its fullness of meaning. With this key in hand the mysteries of the history of this doctrine in the Church are at once solved for us.

One of the chief claims to our attention which Dr. Kuyper's book makes, therefore, is rooted in the fact that it is a product of a great religious movement in the Dutch churches. This is not the place to give a history of that movement. We have all watched it with the intensest interest, from the rise of the Free Churches[90] to the union with them of the new element from the *Doleantie*.[91] We have lacked no proof that it was a movement of exceptional spiritual depth; but had there lacked any such proof, it would be supplied by the appearance of this book out of its heart. Wherever men are busying themselves with holy and happy meditations on the Holy Spirit and His work, it is safe to say the foundations of a true spiritual life are laid, and the structure of a rich spiritual life is rising. The mere fact that a book of this character offers itself as one of the products of this movement attracts us to it; and the nature of the work itself— its solidity of thought and its depth of spiritual apprehension— brightens our hopes for the future of the churches in which it has had its birth. Only a spiritually minded Church provides a soil in which a literature of the Spirit can grow. There are some who will miss in the book what they are accustomed to call "scientific" character;[92] it has no lack certainly of scientific exactitude of conception, and if it seems to any to lack "scientific" form, it assuredly has a quality which is better than anything that even a "scientific" form could give it— it is a religious book. It is the product of a religious heart, and its leads the reader to a religious contemplation of the great facts of the Spirit's working. May it bring to all, into whose hands it finds its way in this fresh vehicle of a new language, an abiding and happy sense of rest on and in God the Holy Spirit, the Author and Lord of all life, to whom in our heart of hearts we may pray:

> Veni, Creator Spiritus,
> Spiritus recreator,
> Tu deus, tu datus coelitus,
> *Tu donum, tu donator.*[93]

Princeton Theological Seminary, April 23, 1900

16

THE 1903 REVISION OF THE
Westminster Confession of Faith
"OF THE HOLY SPIRIT"

The chapter entitled "Of the Holy Spirit", is divided into four sections, which run as follows:

I. The Holy Spirit, the third person in the Trinity, proceeding from the Father and the Son, of the same substance and equal in power and glory, is, together with the Father and the Son, to be believed in, loved, obeyed, and worshipped throughout all ages.

II. He is the Lord and Giver of life, everywhere present in nature, and is the source of all good thoughts, pure desires, and holy counsels in men. By him the prophets were moved to speak the Word of God, and all writers of the Holy Scriptures inspired to record infallibly the mind and will of God. The dispensation of the gospel is especially committed to him. He prepares the way for it, accompanies it with his persuasive power, and urges its message upon the reason and conscience of men, so that they who reject its merciful offer are not only without excuse, but are also guilty of resisting the Holy Spirit.

III. The Holy Spirit, whom the Father is ever willing to give to all who ask him, is the only efficient agent in the application of redemption. He convicts men of sin, moves them to repentance, regenerates them by his grace, and persuades and enables them to embrace Jesus Christ by faith. He unites all believers to Christ, dwells in them as their Comforter and Sanctifier, gives to them the spirit of Adoption and Prayer, and performs all those gracious offices by which they are sanctified and sealed unto the day of redemption.

IV. By the indwelling of the Holy Spirit all believers being vitally united to Christ, who is the Head, are thus united one to another in the Church, which is his body. He calls and anoints ministers for their holy office, qualifies all other officers in the Church for their special work, and imparts various gifts and graces to its members. He gives efficacy to the Word, and to the ordinances of the gospel. By him the Church will be preserved, increased until it shall cover the earth, purified, and at last made perfectly holy in the presence of God.

The Holy Spirit

It will be observed that the several sections of the chapter follow each other logically and develop the doctrine of the Holy Spirit in an orderly sequence. The first sets forth the nature of the Holy Spirit in his relations to the Godhead and to rational creation. The second sets forth his general activities— cosmical, ethical, inspirational, evangelical. The third advances to his specifically soteriological activities and summarizes his work in the salvation of individuals. The last expounds his activities in the Church, by virtue of which the Church is constituted, edified, propagated, and perfected. The doctrine set forth in these several sections is the common doctrine of the Calvinistic churches, and may be found expounded at length in the body of divinity of any standard Calvinistic divine. The chapter is in effect, therefore, a compact summary of the ordinary Calvinistic doctrine of the Holy Spirit and his work.

As this chapter essays to put into brief compass a complete doctrine "Of the Holy Spirit," it necessarily repeats many elements of that doctrine which are already given expression in the Confession; and whenever the Confession has developed any items of this doctrine with fullness, the repetition of them in this chapter is much compressed. The first section of the chapter, for example, merely repeats what the Confession has already said in the following passages:

> "In the unity of the Godhead there are three persons, of one substance, power and eternity,...the Holy Ghost eternally proceeding from the Father and the Son" (II. 3) "Religious worship is to be given to God the Father, Son and Holy Ghost; and to Him alone" (XXI. 2).

The third section is merely a very compressed summary of what the Confession has set forth in minute detail and with exceedingly rich development in that great series of chapters on the Application of Redemption, which constitutes its heart (Chaps. X-XVIII). This summary, certainly, evinces no great firmness or precision of touch. It fumbles a little alike with the conceptions it deals with and with the language in which it clothes them. But it is happily possible to tell the truth even with lisping tongue; and this section manages, even in its somewhat bungling way, to set forth, from the phenomenal or experiential point of sight, a very tolerable account of the progressive stages through which (in the Calvinistic view) a sinner passes as he is brought into the experience of salvation by the Holy Spirit, who is very properly described as "the only efficient agent in the application of redemption."

The several sentences of the fourth section likewise very largely repeat statements which have already found expression in the Confession. The following passages will illustrate this; they follow the order of the sentences in this section:

> All saints that are united to Jesus Christ the Head, by his Spirit and by faith, have fellowship with him, ...and being united to one another in love, they have communion in each other's gifts and graces, and are obliged to the performance of such duties, public and private, as do conduce to their mutual good, both in the inward and outward man (XXVI. 1). The catholic or universal Church, which is invisible, consists of the whole number of the elect, that have been, are, or shall be gathered into one, under Christ the Head thereof; and is the spouse, the body, the fullness of him that filleth all in all (XXV. 1). Unto this catholic visible Church, Christ hath given the ministry, oracles, and ordinances of God, for the gathering and perfecting of the saints, ... and doth by his presence and Spirit, according to his promise, make them effectual thereto (XXV. 3). The grace of faith ... is the work of the Spirit of Christ, ... and is ordinarily wrought by the ministry of the Word: by which also, and by the administration of the sacraments, and prayer, it is increased and strengthened (XIV. 1).

A certain effect of novelty is given to the restatement of the important truths contained in this section, however, by their marshaling in an orderly development of the doctrine of "the Holy Spirit in the Church", and this is increased by the apparent absence from the Confession of any clause embodying, at least with the clearness and emphasis given it here, the inspiring truth enunciated in the last sentence. On the whole, then, this section may fairly be accounted a contribution toward the augmentation of the Confession with new doctrine. The doctrine of the work of the Holy Spirit in the Church is stated in it comprehensively, and not without point. The doctrine of the Church implicated is the common Reformed doctrine, and the statement here given homologates [harmonizes] perfectly with the teaching of the Confession, whether in the main or in subsidiary points.

It is, however, in the second section that the really new matter of this chapter is presented. The second sentence of even this section, to be sure— which, moreover, is out of its logical place— is only a repetition of doctrine already set forth with fullness and emphasis in the First Chapter of the Confession. But the rest of the section is entirely new to the Confession, and gives a comprehensive statement of a great and distinctively Calvinistic doctrine not hitherto incorporated in detailed statement into the Confession— the doctrine, to wit, as it is currently designated by the systematizers, of "Common Grace." This important doctrine, first worked out by Calvin, passed from him into the systems of the Reformed divines in general, to be most richly developed in our own day by perhaps Dr. Charles Hodge[94] and two Dutch theologians who have won the admiration and love of the whole Reformed world by their sturdy support of the Reformed theology in the untoward conditions of present-day Holland— Dr. Abraham Kuyper and Dr. Herman Bavinck.[95]

Of course this distinctively Reformed doctrine was not unknown to the framers of the Confession. It may be found more or less fully expounded in their private writings, and is always adverted to by them with a high sense of its value.[96] It is even incidentally alluded to in the text of the Confession itself.[97] But the framers of the Confession consecrated to it no separate section of their work, and indeed nowhere give it even incidental development. The incorporation of a statement of this doctrine into this chapter is, therefore, a real extension of the Confession by a new doctrinal definition; and the doctrine thus inserted is certainly one of large importance, if not to the integrity of the Calvinistic system or to its full statement for the practical ends of the religious life, yet certainly for its thorough elaboration and its complete development as a comprehensive world-view.

The statement which is here given to this important Reformed doctrine is, from the necessity of the case, succinct rather than elaborated, comprehensive rather than detailed. But it perfectly conforms to the teaching upon this topic of the best Reformed divines. The closeness of its conformity to the ordinary mode of stating the doctrine among accredited Reformed teachers may be fairly estimated by comparing this section with the exposition of the subject by, say, Dr. Shedd[98] or Dr. Charles Hodge. Dr. Hodge, for example, says, among other things:

"God is everywhere present with the minds of men, as the Spirit of truth and goodness, operating on them according to the laws of their own moral agency, inclining them to good and restraining them from evil. . . . To the general influence of the Spirit (or to common grace) we owe all the decorum, order, refinement, and virtue existing among men. . . . The Scriptures speak of God's reasoning with men; of His teaching them, and that inwardly, by His Spirit; of

His guiding or leading them; and of His coming, reproving, and persuading them. These modes of representation would seem to indicate a "moral suasion," an operation in accordance with the ordinary laws of mind, consisting in the presentation of truth and urging of motives. . . . These common influences of the Spirit are all capable of being effectually resisted. . . . We should above all things dread lest we should grieve the Spirit or quench his influence.[99]

The resemblance between such teaching and the statement given in the section of the new chapter before us is patent.

The chapter "Of the Holy Spirit," then, besides reiterating the Confessional doctrines of the nature of the Holy Spirit and of his special activities, on the one hand, in the gift of the Scriptures, and, on the other, in the application of the redemption of Christ to individual sinners, develops and extends the Confessional doctrine of the work of the Spirit in the Church and adds to the Confessional statements the definition of a new doctrine, "Common Grace." In this further development of the one doctrine and fresh formulation of the other, it proceeds in full accord with both the spirit of the Reformed system and the very letter of the most accredited expounder of that system.

17

Holy Ghost or Holy Spirit [100]

Holy Ghost, or **Holy Spirit** [Heb. *Ruach Ha-Elohim* and *Ruach Jehovah;*[101] Gk. *pneuma hagion,*[102] with or without the article, and often without the adjective]: the Spirit of God, of Christ, of Jesus , of the Lord, etc., is the third Person of the Trinity, whose existence, character, and offices are revealed in the Bible. The term "Spirit" in Greek and Hebrew (as in many other languages) means "wind," then "breath," then "life," then the self-conscious, intelligent self-determined, thinking substance of God, angels, and man. The term **to pneuma hagion,** Holy Spirit, in Scripture and Christian theology, does not designate the spiritual substance common to the three Persons of the Godhead, but the third Person or Hypostasis existing in the unity of the substance. A condensed statement will be given (I.) of the scriptural and Church doctrine as to his personality, divinity, procession, and offices; (II.) of the history of opinion on the subject; (III.) of its literature.

I. *The Scriptural and Church Doctrine of the Holy Spirit.*

1. *His Personality*— The attributes of personality are intelligence, will, individual subsistence; and in Scripture all of these are predicated of the Spirit. (1) He uses the pronoun "I," and the Father and Son use the pronouns "he" and "him," when speaking of him (Acts 13:2; John 15:26; 16:13,14); "When he (*ekeivos*) shall come . . . he shall glorify me." (2) His functions all imply distinct personal subsis-

163

tence: he "speaks," "searches," "selects," "reveals," "reproves," "testifies," "leads," "comforts," "distributes to every man as he wills," "knows the deep things of God," "is grieved," etc. (Acts 13:2; 1 Cor. 2:10,11; 12:11; 1 Tim. 4:1). (3) All Christians profess personal allegiance to the Holy Spirit precisely as to the Father and Son. They are baptized *eis to onoma* - into the name of the Father, and of the Son, and of the Holy Spirit (Matt. 28:19). If the two former are Persons, the latter must be. Hence he is our Sanctifier and Comforter. (4) Blasphemy against the Holy Spirit, and the possibility of "resisting," "grieving," and "doing despite to" him, imply his personality (Matt. 12:31,32; Mark 3:28,29; Luke 12:10; Acts 7:51; Heb. 10:29; Eph. 4:30). (5) This has been from the beginning the common faith of all historical churches, and has been given expression in their creeds.

2. His Divinity— (1) He is called by the exclusive names of God. What Jehovah says in the Old Testament the New Testament writers ascribe to the Holy Spirit (cf. Isa. 6:9 with Acts 28:25, and Jer. 31:31-34 with Heb. 10:15; see Acts 5:3,4). (2) Divine attributes are predicated of him: (a) omnipresence (Ps. 139:7; 1 Cor. 12:13): (b) omniscience (1 Cor. 2:10,11): (c) omnipotence (Luke 1:35; Rom. 8:11). (3) Divine works are ascribed to him: (a) creation (Gen. 1:2; Job 26:13; Ps. 104:30); (b) inspiration (Heb. 3:7; 2 Pet. 1:21); (c) miracles (1 Cor. 12:9-11); (d) spiritual regeneration (John 3:6; Titus 3:5). (4) Divine worship is to be paid to him (Matt. 28:19; 2 Cor. 13:14; Matt. 12:31,32).

3. The Procession of the Holy Spirit— This is a technical phrase doubtless originating in John 15:26 ("the Spirit of truth which proceedeth from the Father"), but used by theologians to express the essential relation of the Holy Spirit to the other Persons of the Trinity. The teachings of Scripture and of the whole Church, Roman and Protestant, involve the following points: (1) There is but one God, and he is indivisible. Therefore there is but one indivisible being which is God. (2) This one whole being subsists eternally as three equal Persons, the entire being subsisting as each Person concurrently. (3) The Scriptures reveal (so far forth) the nature and relations of each Person by their names and relative actions. The Father is always first, the Son second, and the Spirit third. The terms Father and Son express eternal reciprocal relation. The Father eternally begets the Son. The Spirit is the infinite personal "Breath" of God, as the Son is his infinite personal "Word." He is the "Spirit of God" and "from God" *(ek tou Theou,* 1 Cor. 2:12) and "the Spirit of the Father," "who proceedeth from the Father" *(para tou patros ekporeuetai,* John 15:26). He is also the Spirit "of the Son" and "of Christ" (Rom. 8:9; Gal. 4:6). He is sent by and acts for the Father; so he is sent by and acts for the Son (John 16:7-14). (4) Thus the Athanasian Creed[103] concludes (paragraphs 20-22), the "Father was made from none, nor created, nor begotten. The Son is from the Father alone, neither made nor created, but begotten. The Holy Spirit is from the Father and the Son, neither made nor created nor begotten, but proceeding." This the Church proposes not as an explanation, but simply as a statement of scriptural data.

The generation of the Son in the Nicene theology[104] is an eternal constitutional (non-volitional) act of the Father, whereby he communicates his whole divine essence to the Hypostasis of the Son, whereby the Son is the "express image of the Father's Person" and "the brightness of his glory." The procession or spiration of the Holy Spirit is a like eternal act of the Father and of the Son, whereby they communicate their whole common substance to the Hypostasis of the Holy Spirit, whereby he becomes their consubstantial personal Breath. As these acts are eternal, they are neither past nor future, but present, without beginning or ending.

4. *His Offices in Nature*— The "Spirit" or personal "Breath" is the Executive of the Godhead, as the "Son" or "Word" is the Revealer. The Spirit of God moved upon the face of chaos and developed cosmos (Gen. 1:2). Henceforth he is always represented as the author of order and beauty in the natural as of holiness in the moral world. He garnished the astronomical heavens (Job 26:13). He is the organizer and source of life to all provinces of vegetable and animal nature (Job 33:4; Ps. 104:29,30; Isa. 32:14,15), and of enlightenment to human intelligence in all arts and sciences (Job 32:8; 35:11; Ex. 31:2-4).

5. *His Offices in Redemption*— Christ promised his disciples on the eve of his crucifixion that he would send them the Spirit of truth as another *Comforter,* **paraklatos,** *Paraclete, Advocatus* (Patron, Counsel, Champion, Helper, etc.; also applied to Christ himself, 1 John

2:1). Although he had been the divine agent effecting the salvation of men ever since Adam, it is said that this Paraclete was not given until after the ascension and glorification of Christ (John 7:39 and Acts 2:32,33); that is, he is now given with a universality, fullness, power, and clearness of manifestation infinitely surpassing that of the past. The present is the dispensation of Spirit in contrast with the preceding preparatory dispensation of law. (1) The Spirit fashioned the body of Christ in the womb of the Virgin, enriched and supported his human soul, and cooperated with him in all the offices he performed in his estate of humiliation (Luke 1:35; Isa. 11:1,2; John 1:32 and 3:34). (2) He inspired the writers of both the Old and the New Testaments as to both thoughts and words (Micah 3:8; 1 Cor. 2:10-13). (3) He teaches those who are spiritually minded the meaning of Scripture (1 Cor. 2:14,15), and applies to all the redemption purchased by Christ (John 16:13,14). Hence he is called the "Spirit of grace" (Heb. 10:29), "of wisdom and understanding" (Isa. 11:2), "of truth" (John 16:13), "of adoption" (Rom. 8:15), "of prophecy" (Rev. 19:10), "of promise" (Eph. 1:13), and "of glory" (1 Pet. 4:14). He regenerates, sanctifies, and preserves the souls and raises the dead bodies of the saints (John 3:6; Rom. 15:16 and 8:11). He is to the Church and to the individual Christian the immanent source of life— *to zoopoion,* the *Life-giver.* (4) He is the bond of life and the organizing principle of the historic Church on earth (1 Cor. 12:13), and Church teachers and rulers are properly only the organs of the Holy Spirit (2 Tim. 1:13,14).

6. *Blasphemy against the Holy Spirit*— (Matt. 12:31,32; Mark 3:29,30; cf. also Heb. 6:4-6 and 10:26,27; 1 John 5:16)— This appears to be an intelligent, deliberate, and malignant "speaking against," and rejection of, the Spirit of grace by one who has been the subject of his full illumination and persuasion. It is never pardoned, because an intelligent preference of sin to holiness and a definite and final rejection of Christ's salvation. See Schaff, *Sin against the Holy Spirit* (1841).

II. History of Opinion on the Holy Spirit.

1. *The State of opinion in the early Church, and the Definition of the Universal Church Doctrine by the Council of Constantinople,* A.D. 381— The Christian Church from the beginning expressed its faith in the terms which were gradually fixed in the (so-called) Apostles' Creed, which acknowledges a Trinity of divine Persons. Nevertheless, the prevalent conceptions were very vague and variable (see testimony of Gregory Nazianzen,[105] *Orat. 31, De Spiritus sancto,* cap. 5), many Church writers regarding the Spirit as more decidedly subordinate to the Son than to the Father. The complete statement of the final faith of the Church was introduced into the Nicene Creed by the Council of Constantinople (A.D. 381) in these words: "And I believe in the Holy Spirit, the Lord, the Giver of Life, who proceedeth from the Father, who with the Father and Son is to be worshipped and glorified, who spake by the prophets." The addition "and the Son" after the words "who proceedeth from the Father" is Western in origin, and was first given conciliar sanction by the Council of Toledo in 589;[106] it has never been accepted by the Greeks. For the most detailed of the universally received definitions, see the Athanasian Creed (circa A.D. 450). These creeds, either in form or substance, have been adopted by historical churches.

2. Heretical Views— Some of the Gnostics considered the Holy spirit and Christ two celestial *Aeons,* generated to restore the disturbed harmony of the Pleroma.[107] The Alogians[108] and other ancient deniers of the divinity of Christ regarded the phrase Holy Spirit as another name for the single person of God. The Sabellians[109] held that it designates one mode of divine operation and the phase of divine revelation peculiar to the present dispensation. The Arians[110] and Semi-Arians[111] regarded the Holy Spirit as the first and greatest creature of Christ, of superangelic but not divine perfection. After the Council of Nicea these parties were called *Macedonians, Pneumatomachi,* and *Tropici.*[112] All modern Arians and Socinians[113] interpret the phrase Holy Spirit as a designation of the energy of God manifested in action. De Wette says the Spirit is God operative in nature; Schleiermacher says he is God operative in the Church.

III. Literature.

Besides the creeds, especially the *Nicene* and *Athanasian Creeds;* and the histories of doctrine, such as Hagenbach's, Shedd's, Neander's; and Schaff's *Histories of the Christian Church;* see especially Owen, *Discourse concerning the Holy Spirit;* Julius C. Hare,

The Holy Spirit

Mission of the Comforter; Parker, *The Paraclete;* Buchanan, *The Office and Work of the Holy Spirit;* Daunt, *Person and Offices of the Holy Spirit;* Kahnis, *Die Lehre vom Heiligen Geist;* Lampe, *Disputationes de Spiritu Sancto;* Smeaton, *The Doctrine of the Holy Spirit;* Swete, *On the History of the Doctrine of the Procession of the Holy Spirit.*

A.A. Hodge
Revised by B.B. Warfield

BOOK
REVIEWS

Review #1 [114]

The Spirit of Christ: thoughts on the indwelling of the Holy Spirit in the believer and in the Church. By Rev. Andrew Murray. (London: James Nisbet & Co., 1888.) Pp. 394, 16mo. The author treats this greatest of all Christian subjects with adequate reverence and tender devoutness, but scarcely with sufficient judiciousness. The mystical spirit has been always of the greatest value to the Church, and sometimes the sole preservative of true Christianity in a materialistic or legalistic age. But no tendency requires a stricter watchfulness to preserve it from extravagance. Mr. Murray's mystical tendency shows itself especially in laying too great stress on the duty of being conscious of the Spirit's working within us, and in an odd insistence on the duty of exercising "faith in the indwelling Spirit" as the source of life— as if the Scriptures proclaimed the necessity of any other faith than that in Christ. Here he introduces an undesirable dualism into the Christian life, finding two moments of development in it corresponding to the two objects of this twofold exercise of faith. He rightly modifies Mr. Boys's statement as to the nature of prayer for the Spirit, and modifies it in the right direction; but it is a great pity that he adopts the confusion of the charismatic and gracious work of the Spirit upon which Mr. Mahan bases his separation of regeneration and sanctification. We must not separate these two works of the Spirit: it is no more true that whom God foreknew, them also he predestinated to be conformed to the image of his Son, and whom he predestinated, them also he called, and whom he called, them also he justified, than it is that whom he justified, them also he glorified, which surely includes more than external acceptance into the heavenly glory. The essence of this passage is to teach that God selects his children, chooses the goal to which he shall bring them, and brings them safely to that goal; and it justifies us in saying that without exception "whom he regenerates, them also he sanctifies." The separation of these two begets the very evil which Mr. Murray deprecates, of failure to live up to our privileges. Enthusiastic minds like Mr. Murray's need to exercise special care in adopting forms of statement from other writers. We meet every now and then in the book with a phrase or a doctrine the implications of which have scarcely been thought through by him. For example, the crude trichotomistic[115] anthropology of p. 34 is an excrescence on his thinking, and is adopted only to be laid aside. On

p. 54 he speaks for a moment like a fully developed Schleiermacherite. And every now and then we strike against a sentence delivered as if it contained the very kernel of the Gospel, which quite puzzles us. For example, what idea of "holiness" underlies the assertion that "It is as the Indwelling One that God is Holy," offered in defense of the statement that the Spirit is "the Holy Spirit" only as sent forth by the incarnate Christ? And what shall we do with the statement made in the same connection, "It is not the Spirit of God as such, but the Spirit of Jesus that could be sent to dwell in us," in the face of the biblical *usus loquendi*[116]? The book is marred everywhere by such straining after novel and striking forms of statement, a vice, we may add, very common with books of this class.

Review #2 [117]

Die Fortdauer der Geistesgaben in der Kirche.[118] Von D. Hermann Cremer. 12mo, pp. 32. (Gutersloh: Verlag von C. Bertelsmann, 1890.) A delightfully written protest against the hunger for miracles showing itself now and again in the Protestant Church, which all those likely to come into contact with the faith-cure fanaticism should read. Dr. Cremer shows that the miraculous gifts were a special privilege of the infant Church, serving a specific purpose in those days of foundation, and are neither to be expected nor wished for now. He shows that this is not to say that the Holy Spirit has deserted the Church of God, or that He no longer endows her with gifts, even extraordinary gifts. It is the lesser that has given way to the greater. The "Wundergaben"[119] are gone, but "Geistesgaben" remain; or, using other terms, the "Wunderzeichen"[120] are gone, but "Wunder" remain; for, in this broader sense, all Christian works are "wonders," and "to help an unsaved soul to saving faith, and to cleanse it of its sins in the name of the triune God, so as that it becomes partaker of the Holy Spirit, and thus to communicate the grace of God from man to man, this is greater than all signs and wonders." And whenever there is an extraordinary work to be done, extraordinary gifts are given to fit for it, and so we have a Luther, and a Spener, and Arnd, a Tholuck, a Fliedner and a Wichern,[121] none of whom did their work in their own strength or by virtue of natural gifts. Nor do we doubt that God is an answerer of prayer: "The prayer-hearing which our Lord Christ promised us is distinguished from miracles, just as the providence of the living God, who has numbered the hairs on our head, is from his special revelations;" and "he who demands miracles as prayer-hearing, runs a great risk of suffering shipwreck of his faith, through his own fault." Dr. Cremer points out the peculiar social difficulties of the day, and the need of extraordinary gifts of God to meet the new conditions, and encourages Christians to pray and hope for them, but not in the way of miracles.

Review #3 [122]

Evidence of Salvation; or, the Direct Witness of the Spirit. By the Rev. Everett S. Stackpole, D.D. 18mo, pp. viii, 115. (New York: T. Y. Crowell & Co. [1894].) The author's zeal is in behalf of the Protestant doctrine of assurance, based upon the testimony of the Holy Spirit. He fears that Christians are learning to do without assurance, and are thus tending to live upon a lowered plane of spiritual attainment; or else are seeking the grounds of certitude in misleading experiences or external reasonings. Either, he perceives, would strike a blow at the roots of Christianity, and practically or logically tend to undermine its supernaturalism. He would draw back men's thoughts to the sealing of the Holy Spirit, and base their assurance upon His supernatural testimony in their hearts. This is a thankworthy undertaking; and it is prosecuted with fervor, knowledge and skill. On one or two points of fundamental importance to the doctrine, however, the author, from his Wesleyan standpoint, is confused and misleading. (1) He does not distinguish clearly and firmly between the witness of the Holy Spirit and the interpretation of that witness by its recipient. His conception vibrates accordingly between salvation and the assurance of salvation as the direct product of that witness. At one time he says: "When we base our salvation upon anything else than this divine testimony in the soul, we have sunk down to the plane of heathen philosophies" (p. 46); and we agree with him heartily, and in this sense accord fully with the statement that "in the days of the apostles no one was considered converted if he were destitute of the direct witness of the Spirit" (p. 61). It is not this that "high Calvinists" doubt: they begin to doubt only when this is transmuted into the proposition that assurance is so of the essence of faith, that faith does not exist where assurance is not present. They draw a distinction between the *certitudo entis* and the *certitudo mentis*[123]— *which* ought not to be a difficult thing to do. "An unconscious reception of the Spirit is a delusion and a snare" (p. 71),

Dr. Stackpole indeed proclaims, with no apparent consciousness of the inevitable "Distinguo"[124] which must be sounding in his ears. No very subtle distinction is drawn when it is suggested that one may be conscious (as every converted man is and must be) of the change that has taken place within him by and through the gift of the Spirit, without being directly conscious that it is the Holy Spirit that has wrought this change. Of this, indeed, no man is directly conscious, seeing that the Holy Spirit works beneath consciousness. Calvinists consentiently witness that it is only by the almighty testimony of the Holy Spirit borne in the heart, that men are persuaded and enabled to believe savingly in Christ: this is only another way of stating their doctrine of "effectual calling," "efficacious grace," or "physical regeneration." But they do not see their way open to affirm that, therefore, no one is saved who has not attained to full assurance that he is saved. Nor is their unwillingness to affirm this founded, as Dr. Stackpole suggests, on a fear on their part lest "if all the elect should receive full assurance, there would be a clear division of the sheep from the goats in their life, and it might lead to practical antinomianism[125]" (p. 61). They heartily wish that all the Lord's people had full assurance. Their unwillingness to affirm it is founded solely upon their perception of the illogical character of the inference. And they are confirmed in their unwillingness to make the step asked of them, by the further perception that those who do make it cannot carry it through. Such sentences as the following show that Dr. Stackpole cannot himself abide by it:

"It would be a mistake to suppose that all Christians at their conversion receive an equally clear and satisfying assurance of divine acceptance' (p.77). 'A really converted person may have erroneous notions about the witness of the Spirit, and so get into despondency. He is not condemned but uncertain' (p. 77). 'A really converted person may have erroneous notions about the witness of the Spirit, and so get into despondency. He is not condemned but uncertain' (p.51). 'He already had all that is essential to the witness of the Spirit, but did not know how to interpret his changed state of heart' (p. 86). 'We do not mean to affirm that the divine testimony is always equally clear. It may be obscured by reason of physical infirmities, temptation, weakness of faith, or ignorance of Gospel promises' (p. 63). 'Some trust tremblingly, waveringly, examining themselves more than looking unto Jesus' (p. 84).

His own personal experience, indeed, as recorded on p. 85 furnishes a clear instance of true conversion without knowledge of it, of salvation existent and persistent without assurance. (2) He misconceives the manner in which the witness of the Spirit is delivered. He represents it as a special revelation, arguing that God will delay neither to forgive a penitent sinner nor "to notify him of the fact" (p. 87). "The general principles of salvation may be found in the written Word," he argues, "but my salvation or yours is nowhere revealed in the Bible. The Word gives no testimony whatever with reference to that event. If I ever learn that for a certainty, it must be by a special revelation to me. The canon of revelation is not completed for me till God has expressly signified to my soul that I am His child" (p. 34). The mode of this revelation is not asserted, however, to be propositional: it comes by way of "spiritual intuition." "So one knows immediately and without reasoning when he feels condemnation for sin, and he knows equally well when that condemnation is removed. Its removal is due to an inwrought conviction that his sins are forgiven. He cannot explain that conviction, neither can he rid himself of it except by voluntary transgression of known moral law" (p. 63). In one word, then, the testimony of the Spirit is conceived of as taking the form of a blind conviction of forgiveness of sins and salvation. How the sinner is to know that this blind conviction is not a delusion, we are not told: we are only told that while one may fancy he has it, when he has it not, yet no one who has it is ever mistaken in it. We miss adequate grounds for this discrimination. We do not see how a blind conviction can testify to anything; we do not see how it can validate itself as a "revelation;" we do not see how God can so deal with rational creatures. By as much as it is reasonable to suppose that God will deal with rational creatures as rational creatures, by so much is it unreasonable to suppose that He will work a conviction of salvation in the minds of His children without cognizable ground. We fall back, therefore, with great confidence upon the common distinction between the "efficient cause" of our assurance and the "formal ground" of our assurance. Assurance is wrought in us by the Holy Spirit, who thus bears His testimony to our salvation; but it is grounded on sufficient reason validated to the intellect. Were it not so, assurance would not even be rational: and if not rational, it would hardly assure, but would inevitably suggest hysteria.

Review #4 [126]

Pneumatologie. oder die Lehre von der Person des heiligen Geistes.[127] Von D. Wilhelm Kölling. 8vo, pp. xxiv, 368. (Gutersloh: C. Bertelsmann, 1894.) Dr. Kölling's bulky treatise on *Theopneustie* was reviewed in this REVIEW for July, 1893 (Vol. iv, p. 487). He almost apologizes for turning aside from that subject, still so much debated, to publish upon the doctrine of the Holy Spirit: critics raising such objections he would have to note that the doctrines of the Word of God and of the Holy Spirit stand very close together, and that a treatise on the Inspirer can readily be deemed only the second volume of one on Inspiration. In days like these, when the very existence of a Holy Spirit is cast so much in doubt and all study of His work so much neglected, the doctrines of His personality and divinity and of His work for the Church and the soul come to rank among those which must above all others be expounded and defended. The historical method of the treatise on Inspiration gives way, however, to a more exegetical one in this treatise— not, however, to the neglect of what has been said by the great masters of this theologoumenon[128]— especially by the three great Cappadocians[129] in the fourth century with reference to the person of the Spirit, and by the great Lutheran trio in the sixteenth century, Gerhard, Chemnitz, Hunnius, with reference to His work. Therefore we are invited to consider in turn the Biblical evidence that the Holy Spirit is a *person*, that He is a *Divine* person and that He shares the intertrinitarian glory; after that we are given a discussion of the "filioque,"[130] and the volume closes with Epilegomena.[131] The work is comprehensive and brings most of the relevant passages and topics under discussion. But we must needs confess that it is dry and formal and little critical, and that the subject is not greatly advanced by its discussions. Perhaps the treatment of the "filioque" is the most satisfying portion of the book. The standpoint of the discussion is soundly orthodox and its witness to the truth consistent and zealous.

Review #5 [132]

The Spirit of Power. As Set Forth in the Book of the Acts of the Apostles. By the Rev. Thomas Adamson, B.D., Glasgow, Formerly Examiner for Divinity Degrees in Edinburgh University. 16mo, pp.

85. (Edinburgh: T. & T. Clark; New York: Imported by Charles Scribner's Sons, 1897.) It seems almost ungracious to subject to strict critical inquiry the basis of a little booklet like this, so obviously well-intentioned, so filled with devout aspirations and so well calculated to elevate its readers into a region of pure enthusiasm for the best gifts and that best gift of all, the Holy Spirit. But the interests of truth require it to be said frankly, but without the least derogation from a sincere sympathy with the object of the booklet or a sincere admiration for the spirit which animates it, that its entire argument is vitiated by primal assumptions which are not only unproven but very clearly invalid. Its whole fabric is built upon the confusion of the extraordinary gift of the Holy Spirit for miracle-working with the ordinary gift of the Spirit for service in the Church; no attempt is made to determine the sense of the phrases which are drawn from Scripture and employed as a basis for the construction made; and the result is naturally a jumble of things that essentially differ. It is quite depressing to observe that so plain a matter may be hidden from even earnest and devout souls, seeking the truth from the very pages of the Word itself; and especially when it is noted that the explicit statements of the eighth chapter of Acts come up for repeated review. But the eighth chapter of Acts is simply an occasion for stumbling for our author. Despite the plain statement of ver. 16 that the Holy Spirit "had as yet fallen upon none of them," he tells us at the opening (p. 12) that "the Samaritan populace after the preaching of Philip" supplies an instance of the "Spirit falling on and filling men at conversion;" and it is not until p. 52 that it dawns on us that he thinks the Samaritans were not "converted" until Peter and John came— although the narrative explicitly says that they had "believed and been baptized" under Philip's preaching (ver. 12). To be sure an attempt is made to adjust this statement to the assertion made: we are told that "they had believed only as Simon Magus did too (viii. 13), with a historical faith which recognized the Messiahship of Jesus and the purpose of God by Him." But of all this there is not a word in the narrative, which rather is a straightforward account of a rich harvest of "conversions," expressed in language as plain and convincing as any account in the Acts. We pass over the apparent slur on "the writer of the Acts himself" on p. 13, and the designation of Simon Magus as a type of "stubborn unbelievers"— which, whatever may

be true of him, he certainly is not represented as being in Acts: as well as the explanation of the reception of the charismata[133] (pp. 51, 52) as dependent on the subjective condition of the subject, whereas a different account is explicitly given in Acts 8:18. The result of this fundamental confusion between extraordinary and ordinary gifts is that the whole argument of the little book goes to pieces. The thing to be shown is true and precious: this way of showing it is a fair model of how it ought not to be done.

Review #6 [134]

The Witness of the Spirit in Relation to the Authority and the Inspiration of Scripture. By William MacLaren, D.D., Professor in Knox College, Toronto. 8vo, pp. 18. (Reprinted from *The Knox College Monthly.* Toronto: F.N.W. Brown, November, 1895.) Nothing would exceed the clearness or thoroughness with which Dr. MacLaren, in this calm and convincing lecture, investigates the doctrine of the Westminster Confession as to the witness of the Spirit to the Scriptures. He shows beyond controversy that the Confession does not rest the authority of Scripture on the witness of the Spirit alone, but on the three concurrent lines of evidence— the external, internal and divine; and that the witness of the Spirit, in the sense of the Confession, is the necessary result of the inward work of the Holy Spirit in opening the eyes of the spiritually blind. And he points out with great force and acumen that while the witness of the Spirit does not itself prove the Bible to be free from error, it should certainly operate greatly to increase confidence in the teaching of the Bible and lead us "to search the Scriptures for the testimony they give and the indications they supply of the nature and extent of their own inspiration." The result of this search, Dr. MacLaren points out, is not doubtful: and thus he would lead those who are inclined to cast the whole weight of the authentication of the Bible's authority on the inner witness of the Spirit to a more adequate conception of the nature and reach of the inspiration of Scripture. The witness of the Spirit validates the authority of the Bible: shall we not accept its own doctrine of inspiration on the authority thus validated?

Endnotes

[1]The title referred to is the superscription "A Psalm of David when Nathan the prophet went to him, after he had gone in to Bathsheba."

[2]Thomas Cheyne (1841-1915) was an OT scholar who was a pioneer in England of the critical approach to the OT. In latter years, some of his views were condemned by scholars as wild and unbalanced.

[3]*totidem verbis* is a Latin phrase which means "in so many words."

[4]A *dictum probans* is "a proof text."

[5]A *genitive absolute* takes place when a noun and participle in the genitive case are not grammatically connected with the rest of the sentence, as is the case in Matthew 9:33; 25:5; and Mark 9:28.

[6]A telic clause is a purpose clause, giving the end or goal of a command.

[7]Epexigetical means "additional words added to give clearer meaning to the preceding words."

[8] George Smeaton was described as "the most eminent scholar of the set of young men who with M'Cheyne and the Bonars sat at the feet of Thomas Chalmers." His excellent work entitled *The Doctrine of the Holy Spirit*, has been made available to this generation by the work of The Banner of Truth Trust, 3 Murrayfield Road, Edinburgh, Scotland EH12 6EL.

[9]This quote is found on pp. 44,45 of the aforementioned book.

[10]The antediluvians were those who lived before (ante) the great deluge (diluvian) at the time of Noah.

[11]By *hypostatical distinctions* Warfield refers to the personal distinctions within the Godhead. The word *hypostasis* is a Greek noun which became the standard designation in Eastern theology of a 'person' of the divine Trinity. It is so used throughout the rest of this chapter.

[12]This is a Latin phrase which means *of one's own accord.*

[13]Isidore of Pelusium (360-440) was born in Alexandria. He was a follower of the teachings of Chrysostom, and held that the Holy Spirit was consubstantial with the Father and the Son.

[14]The word "Shema" is the English transliteration of the first word of the Hebrew text of Deuteronomy 6:4, "Hear..." Jewish tradition describes Deuteronomy 6:4-9, which is called *the Shema,* as fundamental to Jewish belief and duty.

[15]In his monumental work *The History of Redemption*, Jonathan Edwards set forth the fact that from the Fall of man into sin until the Incarnation of Jesus Christ, a period of several thousands of years, the Lord was preparing the world for the coming of the Redeemer of His elect. This work will soon be available through Calvary Press.

[16]The reference to which Warfield here refers is Isaiah 59:19.

[17]Originally from *The Presbyterian and Reformed Review*, v. vi, 1895, pp. 665-687.

[18]*Korinthierbriefe I*, p. 80.

[19]*Hellenism* refers to ancient Greek civilization and its ways of thinking.

[20]Article, "Zur altest. Lehre vom Geiste Gottes," in the *Jahrbb. fur deutsch. Theologie* for 1867, I. p. 9.

[21] These are Genesis, Exodus, Numbers, Judges, 1 and 2 Samuel, 1 and 2 Kings, 2 Chronicles, Nehemiah, Job, Psalms, Isaiah, Ezekiel, Joel, Micah,

Haggai, Zechariah, Deuteronomy and 1 Chronicles may be added, although they do not contain the explicit phrase, "the Spirit of God" or "the Spirit of Jehovah."

[22] These are Leviticus, Joshua, Ruth, Ezra, Esther, Ecclesiastes, Song of Songs, Jeremiah, Lamentations, Hosea, Amos, Obadiah, Jonah, Nahum, Habakkuk and Zephaniah. Proverbs, Daniel and Malachi may, for one reason or another, remain unclassified.

[23] "There is one writer of the Old Testament, in whom all lines and rays of this development come together, and who so stood in the matter of time and of inner manner that they had to come together in this point of unity, if the Old Testament had otherwise found such. This is Ezekiel" (Kleinert, *op. cit.* p. 45). "Isaiah has scattered throughout his prophecies allusions to the Spirit so manifold and various in express descriptions and in brief turns of phrase, that it might not be difficult to put together from his words, the complete doctrine of the Spirit." (Smeaton, *Doctrine of the Holy Spirit,* p. 35).

[24] Fairbairn, *Christ in Modern Theology.* p. 377.

[25] James Denney, *Studies in Theology*, p. 70.

[26] Cf. also the promise of Ezekiel 36:27 and 1 Thessalonians 4:8 (see Toy, *Quotations in the New Testament*, p. 202). Cf. also Luke 1:17.

[27] These words are C.F. Schmid's (*Biblical Theology of the New Testament*, Div. ii. section 24, p. 145, E.T.). Cf. Smeaton, *op. cit.* p. 36: "Events occurring in the moral government of God are (in the Old Testament) also ascribed to the Spirit as the Executive of all the divine purposes."

[28] Kleinert, *op. cit.,* p. 30: "The Old Testament everywhere knows only of an influence of the divine Spirit upon the human Spirit in the interest and sphere of the Kingdom of God, which is in Israel and is to come through Israel." Havernick, *Theologie des alten Testaments*, p. 77: "Of a communication of the Spirit in the narrower sense, after the entrance of sin, there can be question only in the Theocracy." Oehler, *Biblical Theology of the Old Testament*, section 65: "But the Spirit as *the Spirit of Jehovah*, or to express it more definitely *the Holy Spirit of Jehovah* only acts within the sphere of revelation. It rules within the Theocracy."

[29] For example, in the Pentateuch His working is perhaps exclusively cosmical and theocratic-official, (Oehler, *op. cit.* section 65); while His ethical work in individuals is, throughout the Old Testament, more a matter of prophecy than of present enjoyment (Dale, *Christian Doctrine*, p. 317).

[30] Dale, *Christian Doctrine*, p. 318. A striking passage both for its presentation of this fact and for its unwillingness to accept its implications.

[31] Cf. Schultz, *Old Testament Theology*, E. T. ii, 184: "Over the lifeless and formless mass of the world-matter this Spirit broods like a bird on its nest, and thus transmits to it the seeds of life, so that afterwards by the word of God it can produce whatever God wills."

[32] Compare some very instructive words as to this account of creation, by the Rev. John Robson, D.D. of Aberdeen (*The Expository Times,* July, 1894, vol. v. No. 10, pp. 467, *sq.*): "The divine agents in creation are brought before us in the opening of the Book of Genesis, and in the opening of the Gospel of John. The object of John in his Gospel is to speak of Jesus Christ, the Word of God; and so he refers only to His agency in the work of cre-

ation. The object of Moses in Genesis is to tell the whole divine agency in that work; so in his narrative we have the work of the Spirit recognized. But he does not ignore the Word of God; he begins his account of each epoch or each day of creation with the words, 'And God said.' We do not find in Genesis the theological fullness that we do in subsequent writers in the Bible; but we do find in it the elements of all that we subsequently learn or deduce regarding the divine agency in creation . . . Two agents are mentioned: "The Spirit of God brooding on the surface of the waters,' and at each new stage of creative development, the Word of God expressed in the words 'God said' . . . There is thus the Spirit of God present as a constant energy, and there is the Word of God giving form to that energy, and at each new epoch calling new forms into being."

[33]The word *Pantheistic* is an adjective referring to the unbiblical idea that the universe (or *all*) is God.

[34]The word *Cosmotheistic* is also an adjective describing an idea similar to the previous that the cosmos (or *orderly universe*) is God.

[35] Oehler, *Old Testament Theology,* section 65: "But the Spirit as *the Spirit of Jehovah*, or to express it more definitely *the Holy Spirit of Jehovah,* only acts within *the sphere of revelation.* It rules within the theocracy (Isa. 63:11, Hag. 2:5, Neh. 9:20) but not as if all citizens of the Old Testament Theocracy as such participated in this Spirit, which Moses expresses as a wish (Num. 11:29), but which is reserved for the future community of salvation (John 3:1). In the Old Testament the Spirit's work in the divine kingdom is rather that of *endowing the organs of the theocracy with the gifts required for their calling*, and those gifts of office in the Old Testament are similar to the gifts of grace in the New Testament, 1 Cor. 12:1ff."

[36] The idea of communicating to others the Spirit already resting on one occurs again in 2 Kings 2:9, 15, of the communication of Elijah's Spirit (of Prophecy) to Elisha. Cf. Oehler, *Biblical Theology of the Old Testament*, section 65.

[37] Cf. the prayer and endowment of Solomon, in 1 Kings 3.

[38] Compare the cases of the communication of the Spirit, in a different way, in Numbers 11:17,25, 26 and 2 Kings 2:9, 15— already mentioned.

[39] In such passages as Genesis 41:38; Daniel 4:8, 9:18 and 5:11, 14, we have "the Spirit of the Gods" as the equivalent of "the Spirit of God" on the lips of heathen.

[40] Cf. Orelli, *The Old Testament Prophecy*, etc., E. T. p. 11, and also Oehler, *Biblical Theology of Old Testament*, section 65 *ad fin.*

[41] Cf. A. B. Davidson (*The Expositor,* July, 1895, p. 1): "The view that prevailed among the people— and it seems the view of the Old Testament writers themselves— appears to have been this: the prophet did not speak out of a general inspiration of Jehovah, bestowed upon him once for all, as, say, at his call; each particular word that he spoke, whether a prediction or a practical counsel, was due to a special inspiration, exerted on him for the occasion." The statement might well have been stronger.

[42] *Op. cit.* ii, p. 204. The passage is cited for its main idea: we demur, of course, to some of its implications.

[43] In Numbers 14:24 we are told that Caleb followed the LORD fully, "because he had another spirit in him," from that which animated his rebel-

lious fellows. Possibly the Spirit of the Lord may be intended.

[44] Exceptions are found, of course; such as the cases of Balaam, Samson, etc. Cf. H. G. Mitchell, "Inspiration in the Old Testament," in *Christian Thought* for December 1893, p. 190.

[45] Cf. F. H. Woods, in *The Expository Times*, July, 1895, pp. 462-463: "It may be extremely difficult to say what was the precise meaning which prophet or psalmist attached to the phrases, 'the Spirit of God' and 'the Spirit of Holiness." But such language, at any rate, shows that they realized the divine character of that inward power which makes for holiness and truth. 'Cast me not away from Thy presence, and take not the Spirit of Thy holiness from me' (Ps. 51:11). 'And now the Lord God hath sent me, and His Spirit' (Isa. 48:16). 'Not by might, nor by power, but by My Spirit, saith Jehovah of Hosts' (Zech. 4:6). In such passages as these we can see the germ of the fuller Christian thought."

[46] Cf. Psalm 106:13.

[47] See such wonder, nevertheless, expressed by Dr. Dale, in a striking passage in his *Christian Doctrine*, p. 317.

[48] Op. *cit*. ii. p. 184.

[49] Op. *cit.* pp. 55-56.

[50] "Schriftbeweis," i. p. 187.

[51] Cf. Oehler, *op. cit.* section 65, note 5. He looks on Isaiah 43:16 as implying personality and reminds us that the Old Testament prepared the way for the economic Trinity of the new. Cf. also Dale, *Christian Doctrine*, p. 317.

[52] Cf. Dr. Hodge's admirable summary statement: "Even in the first chapter of Genesis, the Spirit of God is represented as the source of all intelligence, order and life in the created universe; and in the following books of the Old Testament He is represented as inspiring the prophets, giving wisdom, strength and goodness to statesmen and warriors, and to the people of God. This Spirit is not an agency but an agent, who teaches and selects; who can be sinned against and grieved; and who, in the New Testament, is unmistakably revealed as a distinct person. When John the Baptist appeared, we find him speaking of the Holy Spirit as of a person with whom his countrymen were familiar, as an object of divine worship and the giver of saving blessings. Our divine Lord also takes this truth for granted, and promised to send the Spirit as a Paraclete, to take His place, to instruct, comfort and strengthen them; whom they were to receive and obey. Thus, without any violent transition, the earliest revelations of this mystery were gradually unfolded, until the Triune God, Father, Son and Spirit, appears in the New Testament as the universally recognized God of all believers" (Charles Hodge, *Systematic Theology*, Vol. I., p. 447).

[53] Op. cit. p. 56.

[54] Cf. Redford, *Vox. Dei.*, p. 236.

[55] Smeaton (*Op. cit.* p. 49) comments on John 7:37 *sq.* thus: "But the Apostle adds that 'the Spirit was not yet' because Christ's glorification had not yet arrived. He does not mean that the Spirit did not yet exist— for all Scripture attests His eternal preexistence— nor that His regenerative efficacy was still unknown— for countless millions had been regenerated by His power since the first promise in Eden— but that these operations of the Spirit had been but an anticipation of the atoning gift of Christ rather than

Endnotes

a GIVING. The Apostle speaks comparatively, not absolutely." Compare further the eloquent words on page 53 with the quotation there from Goodwin.

[56]See the following article which is Warfield's comments on the 1903 Revision of the Westminster Confession of Faith, in which there was the addition of a chapter entitled "Of the Holy Spirit."

[57]Vaughan's fine book has been is available from The Banner of Truth Trust.

[58]Both of these works are also available from The Banner of Truth.

[59]Guers' *Le Saint-Espirit: Etude Doctrinale et Practique* (1865); G. Tophel's *The Work of the Holy Spirit in Man* (E.T., 1882), and also more recently *Le Saint-Espirit; Cinq Nouvelles Etudes Bibliques* (1899).

[60]This title means *The Doctrine of the Holy Spirit.*

[61]See Holtzman,— the *Theolog. Literaturzeitung* of 1896, xxv., p. 646.

[62]This title means *The Biblical Doctrine of the Holy Spirit.*

[63]The "friends of light" were an organization formed in 1841 by ministers within the Prussian state church. The movement tended toward rationalism. Members of the movement soon left the state church, rejected the Apostle's Creed, and adopted as their creed the general statement, "I believe in God and His eternal kingdom as it has been introduced into the world by Jesus Christ."

[64]This Latin sentence means "Clouds of witnesses help more than the unsuitable lights of lightbearing men." The referenced to "lightbearing men" may be a reference to the "friends of light."

[65]Friedrich Schleiermacher (1768-1834) was a German theologian whose writings have had a profound affect upon the world over the past 150 years. He is considered by many to be the father of modern religious liberalism.

[66]Compare the remark of Dr. Smeaton, *op. cit.,* ed. 2, p. 396.

[67]For the epoch-making character of the Reformation in the history of this doctrine compare K. F. Nosgen words, "For its development, a division-line is provided simply and solely by the Reformation, and this merely because at that time only was attention intensely directed to the right mode of the application of salvation. Thus were the problems of the specially saving operation of the Holy Spirit, of the manner of his working in the congregation of believers cast into the foreground, and the theological treatment of this doctrine made of ever-increasing importance to the Church of Christ" (*Geschichte der Lehre vom heiligen Geiste, p. 2*).

[68]For a fuller discussion of this "Second Reformation" of 1886 see Frank Vanden Berg's biography, *Abraham Kuyper,* Wm. B. Eerdmans Publishing Co., 1960, esp. pp. 128-161.

[69]*Schema* is a Latin word meaning "figure, form, fashion."

[70]*Peculium* is a Latin word meaning "private property" or "property Possessed by grant from the father" (i.e. an inheritance). The meaning of this word can be illustrated from an antiquated meaning of the English word "peculiar" in the phrase "a peculiar people." A "peculiar people" means *a people for God's own possession* in the AV of 1 Peter 2:9.

[71]So, for example a careless reading of pp. 65-77 of Pannier's *Le Temoignange du Saint-Espirit* gives the impression of exaggeration, whereas, it is merely the suppression of all minor matters to emphasize the salient facts, that is responsible for this effect.

[72]The phrase "Disruption era" refers to the rending of the Church of Scotland in 1843 over the question of the freedom of the Church to choose their own leaders. Thomas Chalmers was a leading figure in the Disruption and the subsequent formation of the Free Church of Scotland.

[73]These are theological terms: *Theology* is the doctrine of God; *Christology* is the doctrine of Christ; *Anthropology* is the doctrine of man; and *Harmartiology* is the doctrine of sin (from *harmartia,* the Greek word for sin). The word "impetration" means to obtain by request.

[74]Athanasius (about 296-373) was a bishop of Alexandria, Egypt. He defended the deity of Christ and the doctrine of the Trinity against Arius and the Arians.

[75]Anselm (about 1033-1109) was considered a great theologian and was called the "Father of the Schoolmen." Anselm is well known for his interpretation of the atonement, in which he held that the Lord Jesus died on the cross to satisfy the Father. He is also well known for the ontological argument for the existence of God.

[76]"Patristic literature" is literature of the ancient church fathers.

[77]The word "Pelagian" is an adjective describing the doctrines of the British monk, Pelagius, and his followers. Pelagiius lived during the days of Augustine in the early fifth century. The man-centered teachings of Pelagius moved Augustine to oppose these teachings by publishing extensively the doctrines of God's sovereign grace in salvation.

[78]The word "prevenience" means antecedence. In this context, Warfield means by the *prevenience* of grace that God's grace, not man's will or inclination, initiates or begins the work of salvation. God's grace has *efficacy,* i.e. it infallibly secures its object, the salvation of the elect. It has *indefectibility,* i.e. it is free from faults and cannot fail.

[79]The word "vicarious" means substitutionary. Therefore, vicarious atonement is substitutionary atonement. It is the idea that the Lord Jesus Christ suffered in the place of, or in the stead of God's people when He died on the cross.

[80]The Council of Nicea was held in 325 AD. The Council was called by the Emperor Constantine against Arianism. Its' conclusions upheld the teaching of Scripture affirming the full deity of the Lord Jesus Christ. The Nicene Creed that was formulated there said among other things that the Son is "one substance" with the Father (*homoousian*— same substance; not *homoiousian*— similar substance). It also affirmed that the Son was Begotten "not made."

[81]The Council of Chalcedon in 451 concerned the doctrine of the Person of the Lord Jesus Christ. It affirmed that the two natures of our Lord Jesus Christ (divine and human) are unchanged, undivided, and inseparable.

[82]The Synod or Council of Orange was held in 529. It affirmed a weakened Augustineanism and affirmed sacramental grace to overcome innate sinfulness.

[83]See the following context for the meaning of these words "sacerdotal" and "libertarian."

[84]"Sacramentarianism" in this context refers to a very high view of sacraments. Practically speaking, it holds that the sacraments in themselves work effectually for the salvation of the recipient, regardless of his spiritual con-

dition.

[85]The word *media* here is a Latin word which means "that which is intermediate or in the middle."

[86]Semi-Pelagianism is a modified form of Pelagianism (see footnote 77) that perceives man to be weakened spiritually but not dead in trespasses and sins. This teaching denies the total depravity and inability of man. It also denies the doctrine of God's predestination of certain sinners to salvation. It teaches that man, not God, takes the initiative in salvation.

[87]Thomism is the theological tradition which springs from Thomas Aquinas (1224-1274) and his followers.

[88]Tridentinism is the theology which relates to Council of the Roman Catholic Church held in Trent from 1545-1563.

[89]The Latin phrase *soli Deo gloria* means "glory to God alone."

[90]The "Free Churches" here are the churches of the Free Church of Scotland formed by the Disruption in 1843.

[91]The name *Doleantie* comes from the Latin word *doleo* meaning in this context to lodge a legal grievance. It refers to a large group of about 100,000 orthodox, Dutch believers that left the corrupted state Church in 1886 under the leadership of Abraham Kuyper to join with an earlier group to form the second largest Protestant church in the Netherlands, the *Gereformeerde Kerk.*

[92]Thus Beversluis, *De Heilige Geest en zijne werkingen volgens the Schriften des Nieuwen Verbonds* (1896)., speaks of it as Dr. Kuyper's bulky book, which "has no scientific value," though it is full of fine passages and treats the subject in a many-sided way.

[93]The Latin means, "Come, Creator Spirit, Spirit, Restorer, You are God, You have given from heaven, You are the gift, You are the Giver."

[94]Cf. Robert L. Dabney, *Lectures in Systematic Theology,* (Baker Book House, reprinted in 1985), p. 577: "Dr. Hodge expounds with peculiar force and fullness the solemn fact that there is a 'common grace' of the Holy Spirit (which is not 'common sufficient grace')."

[95]Herman Bavinck (1854-1921) was a widely known and respected Dutch Calvinistic theologian. His best known work is his "Reformed Dogmatics" (4 vol.). The first volume, which discusses the doctrine of God, has been translated into English.

[96]Cf., e.g., Twisse, *Riches,* etc., pp. 243, 253.

[97]X. 4. "Some common operations of the Spirit."

[98]W.G.T. Shedd (1820-1894) was a strongly conservative, American, reformed theologian whose major *Dogmatic Theology* (3 vols) is still widely used today.

[99]Cf. Hodge's *Systematic Theology: Vol. 2,* pp. 654-675.

[100]This article was originally written by A.A. Hodge for *Johnson's Universal Encyclopedia* in 1877. It was revised by Warfield for the new edition, NY, 1893-95, vol. 4, pp. 338f.

[101]English transliteration of the Hebrew for "the Spirit of God," and "the Spirit of the Lord."

[102]English transliteration of the Greek "Holy Spirit."

[103]The Athanasian Creed is also called "Symbolicum Quicunque" (Whosoever Symbols) or "Quicunque Vult" (Whosoever will) from the first words

of the Creed. Why it is called "The Athanasian Creed" is not known since it is later than Athanasius. In form it is more a hymn or sermon. It teaches among other things the double procession of the Holy Spirit from the Father and the Son through the Latin phrase *filioque*. The Creed does this in order to assert the equality of the Lord Jesus Christ with the Father and, thus, His deity against the Arians.

[104] Nicene theology is theology that derives from or is harmony with the Nicene Creed. See footnote 80.

[105]Gregory Nazianzen (330-390) was one of the "Three Cappadocians" (Basil of Cappadocia, Gregory of Nyssa, and Gregory of Nazianzen). These three men did very important work concerning the doctrine of the Trinity in the last half of the fourth century.

[106]The Spanish Kingdom of the Visigoths led by the recently-converted King Recared turned from Arianism to the orthodox faith. The Council of Toledo in 589 recognized the orthodox creeds and declared orthodox Christianity to be the state religion.

[107] Both "aeons" and "pleroma" were terms in Gnostic teaching with special meaning. The "aeons" were thought to be eternal, successive emanations from God which mediated between an infinite God and the world. Taken together they constituted the divine "fullness" ("pleroma").

[108]The Alogians (or Alogi) were a sect found in Asia Minor in the late second century. They denied the Gospel of John and its teaching concerning the Logos (cf. John 1:1, 14). They were, therefore, named Alogi by their opponents.

[109]Sabellianism was a movement that began at the beginning of the third century in Asia Minor. It was named after one of its founders, Sabellius. Another name for Sabellianism is modalism. It denied the essential plurality of the Trinity teaching that Father, Son and Holy Spirit are merely three modes of manifestation.

[110]The Arians, disciples of Arius the presbyter of Alexandria (d.336) held that the Lord Jesus is a created being, having had a definite beginning of existence.

[111]The Semi-Arians tried to steer a middle course between the Arians and those who held the orthodox doctrine that the Lord Jesus Christ is of the same essence (homoousian) with the Father. To maintain the idea that the Son is a distinct person they insisted that He has an essence similar (homooisian) to that of the Father.

[112]The name *Pneumatomachi* comes from Greek meaning "fighters against the Spirit." This fourth-century group denied the deity of the Holy Spirit. They held that the Holy Spirit is merely a creature similar to an angel. The name *Macedonians* reflects the name of the leader of the group, Bishop Mecedonius of Constantinople (mid fourth century). Athanasius called a similar group in Egypt *Tropicists* (Tropici). This group explicitly affirmed that the Holy Spirit was of "a different substance" from the Father.

[113]Socinianism was a rationalistic movement begun in the sixteenth century. It became the forerunner of later Unitarianism.

[114]Originally appeared in *The Presbyterian and Reformed Review*, April 1889, pp. 334f.

[115]The word "trichotomistic" is an adjective describing the doctrine of

Endnotes

trichotomy that man is made up of three basic parts (i.e. body, soul and spirit). Most, if not all, reformed students of the Bible hold to the doctrine of dichotomy. This is the view that man is made up of only two major parts, the material body and non-material soul or spirit.

[116]This Latin phrase means "the usual way of speaking."

[117]Originally appeared in *The Presbyterian and Reformed Review*, October 1890, pp. 695ff.

[118]The German title means "The Continuance of the Spiritual Gifts in the Church."

[119]*Wundergaben* are "miraculous gifts."

[120]*Wunderzeichen* are "miraculous signs."

[121]These five godly men mentioned with Luther were greatly used to the glory of God. Their lives span the centuries from the Reformation to Warfield's own day.

[122]Originally appeared in *The Presbyterian and Reformed Review*, July, 1894, pp. 548f.

[123]These two Latin phrases mean respectively the "certainty of the thing" (i.e. objective certainty of salvation) and "certainty of the mind" (i.e. subjective certainty of salvation). See for example Berkhof's *Systematic Theology*, 4th edition and enlarged edition, pp. 507f.

[124]*Distinguo* is the first person singular of the Latin verb meaning "to make a distinction."

[125]The word "antinomianism" comes from two Greek words meaning "against law." It is the teaching that rejects God's moral law for the Christian. Although the word itself is not used in the NT, some accused Paul of this error (Cf. Rom. 3:8; 6:1).

[126]Originally appeared in *The Presbyterian and Reformed Review*, July 1894, pp. 548f.

[127]The title of the Book translated from German into English is *Pneumatology or the Doctrine of the Person of the Holy Spirit.*

[128]The word *theologoumenon* is an English transliteration of a Greek word meaning in this context "a theological discourse or study."

[129]See footnote 105 for a reference to the "three great Cappadaocians."

[130]The Latin word "filioque" means "and through the Son." This word or phrase has important historical and theological significance. It was used to assert that the Holy Spirit proceeds from the Son as well as from the Father. Disagreement over the meaning of this phrase was one of the disagreements that led to the separation of the Western Catholic and Eastern Orthodox wings of the Church. The phrase was not part of the original Nicene Creed but was added later. See also footnote 103 on the so-called Athanasian Creed.

[131]The word *Epilegoumena* is a transliteration of a Greek word simple meaning "epilogue" or "something said in addition."

[132]Originally appeared in *The Presbyterian and Reformed Review*, April 1897, pp. 358,359.

[133]The word *charismata* refers to the gifts of the Holy Spirit.

[134]Originally appeared in *The Presbyterian and Reformed Review*, January 1896, p. 174.

Bibliography

Sermons:

Faith and Life, The Banner of Truth Trust, first reprint 1974
Old Testament Religion, The Conviction of the Holy Spirit,
The Outpouring of the Spirit, The Spirit's Testimony to our
Sonship, The Spirit's Help in our Praying, The Spirit of Faith,
New Testament Puritanism, Spiritual Strengthening, The Sealing
of the Holy Spirit, The Way of Life

The Power of God Unto Salvation, Eerdmans Publishing Co., 1930
The Love of the Holy Spirit, The Leading of the Spirit

Articles:

Selected Shorter Writings of Benjamin B. Warfield: Vol. I,
Presbyterian & Reformed (P & R) Publishing Company, 1970
On the Doctrine of the Holy Spirit: An Introductory Note to
Abraham Kuyper's book, *The Work of the Holy Spirit* (1900).

Selected Shorter Writings of Benjamin B. Warfield: Vol. II,
P & R Publishing Company, 1973
The Confession of Faith as Revised in 1903, The Spirit of God
in the Old Testament (shorter)

Biblical and Theological Studies, P & R Publishing Company, 1968
The Spirit of God in the Old Testament (longer)

Johnson's Universal Encyclopedia, revised edition, N.Y., 1893-95
The Holy Ghost, or Holy Spirit (written with A.A. Hodge)

Reviews:

The Presbyterian and Reformed Review

For an exhaustive bibliography of Warfield's writings see:
A Bibliography of Benjamin Breckenridge Warfield 1851-1921, by
John E. Meeter and Roger Nicole, P & R Publishing Company, 1974

Check website for our latest discounts
Solid Ground Complete Titles Listing
Newest Titles in Bold

Addresses to Young Men by Rev. Daniel Baker $16.00

Advice to a Young Christian by Jared B. Waterbury $15.00

The Afflicted Man's Companion by John Willison $20.00

Anecdotes: *Religious, Moral & Entertaining* by Charles Buck $28.00

Annals of the American Baptist Pulpit, W.B. Sprague $100.00 2 vols. (HC)

Annals of the American Presbyterian Pulpit, W.B. Sprague $215.00 3 vols. (HC)

Assurance of Faith, - Louis Berkhof $11.00

At the Evening Hour & Thoughts for Young Men by E.D. Warfield & J.C. Ryle $18.00

Backslider, The: *Nature, Symptoms & Recovery* by Andrew Fuller $13.00

Be Careful How You Listen: *Getting the Most out of the Sermon* by Jay Adams $16.00

Bible Animals: *And the Lessons Taught by Them for Children*, Richard Newton $16.00

Bible Jewels: *And the Lessons Taught by Them for Children*, Richard Newton $16.00

Bible Models: Shining Lights of Scripture by Richard Newton $32.00

Bible Promises: *Sermons for Children* by Richard Newton $17.00

Bible Warnings: *Sermons for Children* by Richard Newton $25.00

Biblical &Theological Studies, - Princeton Profs. (HC) $60.00 , (PB) $40.00

Body of Divinity by Archbishop James Ussher (HC) $50.00

Bow in the Cloud *Springs of Comfort in Affliction* by Buchanan, etc., $25.00

My Brother's Keeper: *Letters to a Younger Brother* – J.W. Alexander $13.00

Bunyan of Brooklyn: *Life and Practical Sermons of* Ichabod Spencer $30.00

Calvinism in History - Nathaniel McFetridge $13.00

Calvin Memorial Addresses – Warfield, Webb, Orr, Reed, D'Aubigne... $25.00

Calvin on Scripture & Divine Sovereignty by John Murray $12.00

Chief End of Man, The by John Hall $12.00

Child at Home, The - John S.C. Abbott $15.00

Child's Book on the Fall of Man, The by Thomas H. Gallaudet $11.00

Child's Book on Repentance, The by Thomas H. Gallaudet $13.00

Child's Book on the Sabbath by Horace Hooker $16.00

Child's Book on the Soul by Thomas H. Gallaudet $15.00

Christian Pastor, The *Office & Duty of* Stephen H. Tyng $14.00

Christian's Present for All Seasons: *Thoughts of Eminent Divines* - $38.00

The Christian Warfare by John Downame $45.00

Christ in Song - Compiled by Philip Schaff $40.00

Christ on Cross & The Lord our Shepherd – John Stevenson $40.00

Church of Christ: In Two Volumes by James Bannerman $75.00

Church Members Guide – John Angell James $16.00 pb.; $27.00 hc.

Phone 205-443-0311 – www.solid-ground-books.com

Check website for our latest discounts

Classic Reformed Discourses & Essays by J.H. Merle D'Aubigne $30.00

Come Ye Apart: *Thoughts from Gospels* – J.R. Miller $25.00

Commentaries on Galatians-Thess. By John Eadie $145.00 (5 vols)

Commentary on Hebrews by William Gouge, $115 hc, $85.00 pb (2 vols.)

Commentaries on Joshua, 1 & 2 Samuel by William G. Blaikie $92.00 (3 vols)

Commentary on the Epistle to the Romans by W.G.T. Shedd $32.00

Commentary on the New Testament by John Trapp $80.00

Commentary on the Pastoral Epistles by C.J. Ellicott $20.00

Commentary on Second Peter by Thomas Adams HC $90.00

Commenting and Commentaries by C.H. Spurgeon $16.00

Common Faith, Common Culture by Joseph Bianchi $16.00

Communicant's Companion, The by Matthew Henry $20.00

Decisional Regeneration vs. Divine Regeneration by J.E. Adams $8.00

Devotional Life of a Sunday School Teacher, The – J.R. Miller $12.00

Divine Love, The: *12 Sermons on God's Love* by John Eadie $28.00

The Divine Purpose *Displayed in Providence & Grace* by John Matthews $16.00

The Doctrine of Endless Punishment by W.G.T Shedd $15.00

Doctrine of Justification by James Buchanan $35.00

Doctrine of Sovereign Grace Opened & Vindicated by Isaac Backus $15.00

Duties of Church Members & Plea to Pray for Pastors by James & Spring $5.00

Early Piety Illustrated: *Memoir of Nathan Dickerman* by Gorham Abbott $11.00

Essays on the Old Testament and Pentateuch by Robert Dick Wilson $32.00

Evangelical Truth: *Sermons for the Family*– Archibald Alexander $36.00

The Excellent Woman: *As Portrayed in Proverbs* – Anne Pratt $20.00

Exposition of the Baptist Catechism by Benjamin Beddome $17.00

Exposition of the Epistle of Jude by William Jenkyn $55.00 (hc)

An Exposition of the Ten Commandments by Ezekiel Hopkins $28.00

Expository Discourses on the Book of Genesis by Andrew Fuller $40.00

Expository Lectures on Ruth and Esther by George Lawson $25.00

Family Worship for the Christmas Season by Ray Rhodes $12.00

Family Worship for the Reformation Season by Ray Rhodes $12.00

Family Worship for the Thanksgiving Season by Ray Rhodes $12.00

Famous Missionaries of the Reformed Church by James I. Good

Famous Reformers of the Reformed & Presbyterian Church by J.I. Good

Famous Women of the Reformed Church by James I. Good $22.00

The Family at Home: *Illustrations of Domestic Duties* by Gorham Abbott $25.00

The Fear of God: *The Soul of Godliness* by John Murray $5.00

Feed My Lambs: *Lectures to Children* by John Todd $15.00

First Things: *Discourses from Genesis* – Gardner Spring $50.00

Phone 205-443-0311 – www.solid-ground-books.com

Check website for our latest discounts

Five Points of Calvinism by Robert L. Dabney $10.00

Forgotten Heroes of Liberty, The by J.T. Headley $27.00

For Whom Did Christ Die? *The Extent of the Atonement* by John Murray $5.00

Friendship: The Master Passion by H. Clay Trumbull $25.00

From the Flag to the Cross: *Civil War Stories* by A.S. Billingsley, $34.00

From the Pulpit to the Palm-Branch: *Memorial to Spurgeon* $25.00

From Toronto to Emmaus: *Empty Tomb Skepticism to Faith* by James White $17.00

Gadsby's Hymns: *Selections of Hymns for Worship* by William Gadsby $20.00

Gentleman and a Scholar – J. A. Broadus (HC) $40.00; (PB) $30.00

Golden Hours: *Heart-Hymns of the Christian Life*– Elizabeth Prentiss $10.00

Good, Better, Best: *Classic Work on Ministry to the Poor* by J.W. Alexander $17.00

Grace and Glory: *Sermons from Chapel at Princeton Seminary* Geerhardus Vos $15.00

Harmony of the Divine Attributes *in the Work of Redemption* by Wm Bates $28.00

Hawker's Poor Man's N.T. Commentaries (HC) (3 vols.) $195.00

Hawker's Poor Man's O.T. Commentaries (HC) (6 vols.) $395.00

Hawker's Poor Man's Bible Dictionary (HC) by Robert Hawker $55.00

Heart for Missions, A: *Life of Samuel Pearce* by Andrew Fuller $17.00

Heaven Upon Earth: *Jesus, Best Friend in Worst Times,* James Janeway $23.00

Heroes of the Early Church by Richard Newton $17.00

Heroes of Israel: *Abraham – Moses* by William G. Blaikie $35.00

Heroes of the Reformation: *Lessons for Young* by Richard Newton - $20.00

History of Christian Doctrine (2 vols) by William G.T. Shedd $62.00

History of Preaching (HC) (2 vols.) - Edwin C. Dargan $115.00

History of the Sufferings of the Church of Scotland – Robert Wodrow $250.00

Homiletics and Pastoral Theology – William G.T. Shedd $22.00

The Humanness of John Calvin by Richard Stauffer $13.00

Imago Christi: *The Example of Christ* – James Stalker $18.00

The Influence of the Bible on Mind & Character by John Matthews $18.00

Is the Mormon my Brother? By James R. White $20.00

Italian Reformer, The: *Aonio Paleario* by W.M. Blackburn $23.00

JEREMIAH: A Parable of Jesus by Douglas Webster $15.00

Jesus and I are Friends: *Life of J.R. Miller* – John Faris $19.00

Jesus of Nazareth: *Character, Teachings & Miracles* by John Broadus $11.00

Jesus the Way: *A Child's Guide to Heaven* – Edward Payson Hammond $11.00

Jewish Tabernacle: *In Its Typical Teaching* by Richard Newton $25.00

King's Highway, The: *10 Commandments for the Young* R. Newton $20.00

Lectures on the Acts of the Apostles by John Dick $32.00

Lectures on the Bible to the Young by John Eadie $16.00

Lectures on the Book of Esther by Thomas M'Crie $25.00

Phone 205-443-0311 – www.solid-ground-books.com

Check website for our latest discounts

Lectures on the History of Preaching – John A. Broadus $19.00

Lectures on the Law and the Gospel by Stephen Tyng $25.00

Lectures on Revivals of Religion by William B. Sprague $25.00

Legacy of a Legend: *Spiritual Treasure from the Heart of Edward Payson* $10.00

Let the Cannon Blaze Away by Joseph P. Thompson $23.00

Letters to a Mormon Elder by James R. White $20.00

The Life & Letters of James Henley Thornwell by Benjamin M. Palmer $60.00

The Life & Letters of James Renwick: Scots Martyr by WH Carslaw $20.00

Life and Sermons of Ichabod Spencer (HC) (3 vols.) $120.00

Life of Jesus Christ for the Young by Richard Newton $65.00 (2 vols.)

Light at Evening Time: *Support & Comfort of the Aged* $25.00

Little Pillows and Morning Bells by Francis Havergal $16.00

Lives, Our Fortunes & Our Sacred Honor, Our by Charles Goodrich $30.00

Log College: *Accounts from the Great Awakening* by Archibald Alexander $20.00

Lord of Glory: *Classic Defense of the Deity of Christ* - B.B. Warfield $18.00

Luther's Scottish Connection by James McGoldrick 17.00

Madison Ave. Lectures on Baptist Principles & Practice by Weston $25.00

The Man of Business by J.W. Alexander, W.B. Sprague, John Todd etc. $20.00

A Manual for the Young: *Exposition of Proverbs 1-9* by Charles Bridges $13.00

The Marrow of True Justification by Benjamin Keach $12.00

Martyrland: *A Tale of the Covenanters* by Robert Simpson $20.00

Mary Bunyan: *Faith of the Blind Daughter of John Bunyan* by S.R. Ford $20.00

Memorial Tributes: *Funeral Addresses* by Spurgeon, Newton, Jay $35.00

The Minister and His Greek New Testament by A.T. Robertson $14.00

The Missionary Enterprise: 15 Discourses, edited by Baron Stow, $23.00

The Mission of Sorrow: *God's Purpose in Afflictions* by Gardiner Spring $11.00

More Love to Thee: *Life of Elizabeth Prentiss* – GL Prentiss (PB) $35.00; HC $50.00

Mothers of the Wise and Good - Jabez Burns $16.00

Mother at Home, The – John S.C. Abbot $15.00

Mourning a Beloved Shepherd – Charles Hodge & John Hall $10.00

Morning Stars: *Names of Christ for His Little Ones* by Francis Havergal $12.00

My Mother: *Recollections of Maternal Influence* – John Mitchell $20.00

National Preacher, The – Edited by Austin Dickinson $23.00

Notes, Critical & Explanatory on the Acts of the Apostles by Jacobus $32.00

Notes on Galatians by J. Gresham Machen $20.00

Nuts for Boys to Crack: *Earthly Stories w/ Heavenly Meaning* by John Todd $20.00

Old Paths for Little Feet – Carol Brandt $13.00

Opening Scripture: *Hermeneutical Manual* – P.Fairbairn HC $50.00; PB $35.00

Opening Up Ephesians Peter Jeffery $9.00

Phone 205-443-0311 – www.solid-ground-books.com

Check website for our latest discounts

A Short Explanation of Hebrews by David Dickson $13.00

Shorter Catechism Illustrated by John Whitecross PB - $15.00; HC $25.00

Small Talks on Big Questions: by Helms & Thompson-Kahler $32.00

Soldier's Catechism: *For US Armed Forces* by Michael Cannon $15.00

Southern Presbyterian Pulpit: *Expository Sermons* by Dabney, Hoge, Palmer $30.00

Speaking the Truth in Love: *Life of Roger Nicole* by David Bailey $34.00

The Sovereignty of God by John Murray, John Macleod et. $18.00

Stepping Heavenward (HC) – Elizabeth Prentiss $25.00

Stepping Heavenward Study Guide – Carson Kistner $14.00

Still Hour, The: *Communion with God in Prayer* by Austin Phelps $12.00

Sunday School Teachers Guide – John Angell James $11.00

Theology on Fire: 1 & 2 – Sermons of J.A. Alexander $28.00 each

THEOLOGY: *Explained & Defended* by Timothy Dwight $225.00 set (4 vols) HC

Theological Interpretation of American History by C. Gregg Singer $25.00

Thoughts on Preaching by James W. Alexander $22.00

The Tract Primer: *First Lessons in Sound Doctrine* by American Tract Society $11.00

Transfigured Life, The: *Selected Shorter Writings of JR Miller* $25.00

The Travels of True Godliness by Benjamin Keach $17.00

Truth About Christmas, The – Peter Jeffery $4.00

Truth & Life: *22 Christ-Centered Sermons* by Charles P. McIlvaine $30.00

Truth Made Simple: *Attributes of God for Children* by John Todd $15.00

The TRUTH Set Us Free: 20 Nuns Tell Their Stories by Richard Bennett $16.00

Two Men from Malta: *Passionate Appeal to Roman Catholics* by Joe Serge $15.00

An Undivided Love: *Loving and Living for Christ* by Adolphe Monod $15.00

What is the Kingdom of God? By R.C. Reed $12.00

Whatsoever Things Are True: *Discourses on Truth* – J.H. Thornwell $16.00

Withhold Not Thine Hand: *Evening Sermons* by William Jay $35.00

Woman: Her Mission and Life – Adolphe Monod $12.00

Word and Prayer, The: *Devotions from the Minor Prophets* – John Calvin $11.00

The Workman: *His False Friends & True Friends* by Joseph P. Thompson $20.00

Work of the Ministry, The – William G. Blaikie - $22.00

THE WORKS OF THOMAS MANTON (22 vols) HC $1,000.00

Yearning to Breathe Free? *Immigration, Islam & Freedom* by David Dykstra $16.00

Young Ladies Guide – Harvey Newcomb $22.00

Young Peoples' Problems by J.R. Miller $16.00

Youth's Book on Natural Theology by Thomas H. Gallaudet $18.00

Origin of Paul's Religion, The by J. Gresham Machen $24.00

Orthodoxy and Heterodoxy: *Writings on Theology & Ethics* – W.G.T. Shedd $23.00

Our Sovereign God by Boice, Packer, Stott, Sproul, Nicole $16.00

Pardon and Assurance by William J. Patton $20.00

Pastor in the Sickroom – John Wells $13.00

A Pastor's Counsel by Jonathan Edwards, Thomas Scott etc. $12.00

Pastor's Daughter, The – Louisa Payson Hopkins $16.00

Pastor's Sketches: Double-Volume Work– Ichabod Spencer $35.00

Pathway into the Psalter by William Binnie $30.00

Paul the Preacher: *Discourses in Acts* by John Eadie $30.00

Person and Work of the Holy Spirit, The – B.B. Warfield $12.00

The Power of the Pulpit by Gardiner Spring $20.00

Power of God Unto Salvation – B.B. Warfield PB - $18.00; HC $32.00

Preacher and His Models, The – James Stalker $19.00

Precious Seed: *Discourses by Scottish Worthies* by Brown, Chalmers, $32.00

Princeton Sermons from 1891-92 by Hodge, Warfield, Patton etc.

Publications of the American Tract Society, 6 vols. $175.00

Preparation and Delivery of Sermons: *Dargan Edition* – J.A. Broadus $35.00

Psalms in History and Biography, The by John Ker $18.00

Psalms in Human Life by Roland Prothero $25.00

Pulpit Crimes: *Criminal Mishandling of God's Word* by James White $17.00

Rays from the Sun of Righteousness: *Sermons for Children* by Richard Newton $17.00

Redeemer's Tears Wept Over the Lost, The by John Howe $11.00

Repentance & Faith: *Explained to the Young* by Charles Walker $16.00

Sabbath Scripture Readings: *New Testament* by Thomas Chalmers $32.00

Sabbath Scripture Readings II – Old Testament by Thomas Chalmers $35.00

Safe Compass and How it Points: *Sermons to Children* by Richard Newton, $16.00

Scottish Pulpit, The – William M. Taylor $19.00

Scientific Investigation of the Old Testament by Robert Dick Wilson $18.00

Scripture Biography for the Young: Vols. 1 - 5 by T.H. Gallaudet $95.00

Scripture Biography for the Young: King Josiah by T.H. Gallaudet $12.00

Scripture Guide, The – J.W. Alexander $18.00

Secret of Communion with God – Matthew Henry $12.00

Secrets of Happy Home Life by J.R. Miller $5.00

SEEKING GOD: *Do You Really Want to Know God?* by Peter Jeffery $5.00

Sermons for Christian Families by Edward Payson $20.00

Sermons to the Natural Man – William G.T. Shedd $24.00

Sermons to the Spiritual Man– William G.T. Shedd $24.00

Shepherd's Heart, A – Pastoral Sermons of J.W. Alexander $28.00

Phone 205-443-0311 – www.solid-ground-books.com

CPSIA information can be obtained
at www.ICGtesting.com
Printed in the USA
BVHW07s1957041018
529186BV00001B/195/P